Market Timing

3rd Edition

Tony Pow

Why you want to read this book

It should improve your financial health substantially. There are about a million investment books. Why we need another one?

- This book has about 180 pages (6*9). It covers most topics in market timing.

- A best seller with many editions written by a Ph.D. has all the convincing fundamental reasons why there will be a market crash with all kinds of bubbles going to burst. If you followed the book that was published in 2009, you are losing the potential profits from 2009 to today (2016). I bet you cannot time the market without technical analysis.

- There are books written by predictors on the market such as the Dow 40,000 and the popular 'coming' market crash book published around 2009. Some have decent predictions, but check how many right predictions they have since the right one. Usually none! It is usually their one-trick pony.

- This book's chart has detected the last two market crashes correctly. It will work as in the next market crash. However, it may not give us ample timing to prepare to sell our stocks like the last two. However, it is far profitable to use the simple, free chart than without.

  I also included how to detect market plunge without any chart. Just enter SPY or any ETF that represents the market. If the SMA-200% is less than zero, there is a good chance the market is plunging. There are many other supporting hints.

- Check out my success stories.
  http://tonyp4idea.blogspot.com/2015/09/successes.html

- This book is not a novel or documenting the story of my life. All related chapters are grouped in a section for easy future reference. Some chapters are not easy to digest as they have a lot of pointers and some may require you to try them out you.

Contents

Filler 12 noon is not 12 pm

The Chinese restaurant I went to says they are open at 12 am. Are they wrong or is the world wrong?

The next hour after 11 am is 12 am, NOT 12 pm. The one who set it up did it totally wrong and no one complains about it until now. If I were born earlier, I would have corrected it.

Highlights

My motivation to write this book

I would like to share my experiences, both good and bad. I use simple-to-follow techniques using the free (or low-cost) resources available to us. I have been successful in investing for decades. I am enjoying a comfortable financial life. I do not hold back my 'secrets' as my children are not interested in investing. I offer you a small legacy in sharing my investing ideas.

If you are looking at how to make a 100% return overnight, there are many other books claiming to do so, and then this book is not for you. This book describes how to be a 'turtle' investor making a fortune gradually and surely. Before you begin, first define your objectives.

My steps to trade stocks (ETFs are far simpler)

1. Search for valued stocks (there are many strategies to choose from).
2. Evaluate the screened stocks by
    a. Fundamental Analysis.
    b. Intangible Analysis.
    c. Qualitative Analysis.
    d. Technical Analysis.
3. Sell stocks.
    Every 6 months (shorter duration for some strategies), perform the same as in Step #2 to determine whether you need to sell the stocks you own, or just keep them for another 6 months.

The power of market timing

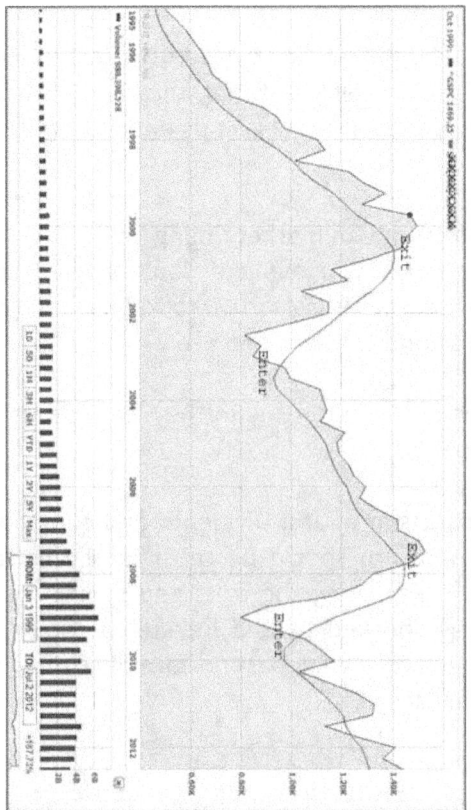

Most e-book readers allow you to select the graph to make it fit entirely on your screen. I use SPY, an ETF simulating the market. Detecting market plunges as seen in this graph indicates the exit points and reentry points also from 2000 to 9-2009 as follows.

Market Plunge	Peak	Bottom	Indicator Exit	Indicator Reenter
2000	08/28/00	09/20/02	10/01/00	06/01/03
2007	10/12/07	03/06/09	02/01/08	09/01/09
			08/01/11	11/01/11

Table: Vital Dates

For simplicity I skipped a few brief exits and reentries since 2011. You can run the simple chart once a month. When it indicates a potential market plunge is close, run the chart once a week. The last row represents a false signal.

This is based on stock prices so it may not identify the peaks and bottoms precisely, but so far it has not failed to avoid big losses and ensure big gains by reentering the market. I hope the next market plunge will most likely give us enough time to act as these two did.

Unbelievable return with market timing

Calculate how much you made if you followed the above exit points and reenter points from 2000 to today. I bet you would have made a good fortune.

I compared the above returns with the SPY without market timing from 1-2000 to 9-2013.

There are many assumptions. Dividends and compounding are not considered. My return should be substantially better if I include buying contra ETFs during the exits and selling them during the reentries. I was shocked by the incredible return by using this simple market timing. Again, past performance does not guarantee future performances.

Summary info:

S&P 500 1-2000 to 9-2013	With Market Timing	Without Market Timing
Better	**500%**	
Gain	1,000	167
Gain %	68%	11%
Annualized gained	5%	1%
Days	4,959	4,959

Calculations:

S & P 500	With Market Timing	Without Market Timing
1-2000	1,469[1]	1,469[1]
Exit 10/01/00	1,041[2]	1,041
Enter 06/01/03	1,041	964[4]
Exit 02/01/08	1,489[3]	1,379[4]
Enter 09/01/09	1489	1,020[5]
Exit 08/01/11	1,888	1,293
Enter 11/01/11	1,888	1,251
09/03/13	2,469	1.638
Gained	2,469 − 1,469=1,000	1,638-1,469=167

Gain %	1000/1469 = 68%	167/1469 = 11%
Annualized gained	68% * 365/4959=5%	11%*365/4959=1%
Better	(1,000-167)/167 = 500%	

Portfolio with Market Timing:

[1] Both start with S&P 500 of 1,469 on 1-3-2000.

[2] 10/01/00

The market timing portfolio exits the market and remains the same value of 1,041 until 6/1/00.

[3] 02/01/08

The market timing portfolio exits the market and remains the same value of 1,489 until 9/1/09.

'1,489' is calculated as follows:

1,041 * (1 + Rate) = 1,041 * (1 + 1,379-964)/964) = 1,489

where the S&P 500 is 964 on 6/1/00 and 1,379 on 2/1/08.

The other calculations are based on the S&P 500 at 1,020 on 9/1/9, 1,293 on 8/1/11, 1,251 on 11/1/11 and 1,636 on 9/3/13.

Portfolio without Market Timing:

[1] Both starts with the S&P 500 of 1,469 on 1-3-2000. We could use the 9/3/13 the S&P 500 value, but it would not account for some compounded interest considerations.

[4] S&P 500 is 964 on 6/1/00 and 1,379 on 2/1/08.

[5] 02/01/08. The portfolio value is calculated to be 1,020 as follows:

1,379 * (1 + Rate) = 1,379 * (1 + (1020-1379)/1379) = 1,020

where S&P 500 is 1,379 on 2/1/08 and 1,020 on 9/1/09.

The other calculations are based on the S&P 500 at 1,293 on 8/1/11, 1,251 on 11/1/11 and 1,636 on 9/3/13.

I cannot believe the shocking return with market timing. I checked my calculations and there was nothing wrong that I could find. If you find something wrong, send your findings to me (pow_tony@yahoo.com).

Even if I made a mistake somehow and got 100% instead of 500%, it still doubles the return without market timing! Ask any fund manager what it means to his or her fund performance and his / her career.

My simple technique that does not use chart told us to **exit the market** on around March 20, 2022.

Bubbles

Bubbles have existed throughout our history. Bubbles occur due to the excessive valuation most likely driven up by the big institutional investors (fund managers, pension managers, hedge fund manager, etc.). Asset valuations are then driven even higher by the retail investors. For example in 3/2014, the market bubble was caused by the government stimulus with the injection of capital into the excessive money supply and subsidies. The first investors riding the wave made good money, and the last ones buying at the peak will lose.

From our recent history, we have the 2000 internet bubble, and then the 2007 (2008 for some) housing bubble. The chapter "Spotting Big Market Plunges" illustrates it was easy to detect the last two plunges. It could save us more than 25% of your portfolio in the next plunge.

Today most of the mentioned bubbles could be caused by pumping too much money into the economy by the government. However, the government cannot keep on injecting money into the economy, and ask our children to pay for our debts forever. When the injections stop, the market will drop fast and deep.

USD

As of mid-2020, the USD is doing quite well. It could be the other countries (EU and Japan) are doing worse than us, as Einstein said, "everything is relative". The strong USD is not good for exports and the global corporations would have less profits after converting them back to USD. However, the excessive printing and high government debts would shake the status of USD as a reserve currency. It will also be hurt if China sells the U.S. Treasury bonds she owns.

Bond

The bond bubble will burst when the interest rates rise. Also it will as the interest rates should have been bottomed by as of mid-2020. It is possible that it could go negative.

Stocks

There are several bubble stocks such as FAANGs. The market was peaking in Jan., 2020 before the virus breakout. Play defense with stop loss orders. The record of margin debt is a big concern. When the credit is tightened with higher interest rate, this bubble will burst.

When to act

Without a time machine, no one can pinpoint when most of these bubbles will burst. Your timing to act depends on your risk tolerance, your knowledge and your greed.

Today, we have the housing bubble (2007-2008), the gold bubble, the market bubble, the second housing bubble, the debt bubble, the bond bubble, the second market bubble, etc. It seems like we can never get out of the bubble cycle. In 2020, the world would be in a global recession if the trade war between the two largest economies continue. It would be worse if the trade war turns into a military war.

Since the world is economically connected better than before. When the U.S.A. sneezes, it affects our trading partners such as European countries along with China and Japan, and also their partners such as the resource-rich countries of S. America, Australia, Russia, Canada and Africa.

For me, it is safer not to try to make the last buck when the reward / risk ratio is too low. A good sleep would improve your health which is worth all the gold in the world.

How to beat the S&P 500 index by 100%

I recommended 20 stocks in an article Amazing Return in Seeking Alpha, a website for investors. If you bought them on the published date and then you would have beaten the S&P 500 index by over 100% without considering dividends as demonstrated in my other article A Tale of Two Portfolios. One of the many techniques is my Pow P/E as illustrated in another article The Mysteries of P/E.

Let's say I made a mistake and it is only a 10% gain. How many fund managers can beat the S&P 500 index by 10% regularly?

Introduction

No one including all the Federal Reserve chairmen / chairwomen and all the Nobel-Prize winners in economics can predict market plunges. Many predicted correctly market crashes by pure luck and some even received Nobel Prizes and became famous. Our simplest technique told us to exit the market on around March 20, 2022.

There is no model and formula to predict market plunges except my simple chart described in this book. It works for the last two market plunges and hopefully it will work for the next market plunge but it may give us ample time to prepare as the last two. This new edition includes a technique that does not require charting.

The chart depends on the falling stock prices, so it will not detect the bottoms and peaks precisely, but it will prevent further losses and reenter the market for larger gains. The chart is very simple to use and there is nothing to buy or subscribe to.

We would make far more money when selling at the peak and buying at the bottom. There are some common parameters in the last two market peaks / bottoms.

They are all common sense to me. The chart could be the best-kept secret. I guess most folks do not want to share this shocking tool to detect market crashes.

I have spent a lot of time looking for hints to detect market plunges. This could help you avoid the next big plunge that could cost you more than 30% of your investment. Market recoveries offer the best opportunity to make big money, and in this book, I describe when and how. Your money to buy this book and the time you invest in reading it could lead to huge gains. Such diligence and effort keeps on rewarding for years to come.

I have been a stock investor for over 30 years and a full-time investor for the last seven years with exhaustive stock research and performance improvements. This book is targeted to retail investors and I am one myself.

I predict that a secular bull market will be starting as early as 2017 when the two wars will finally be totally over. If the wars do not end as expected, most likely it will still happen before 2020. I have strong arguments for both scenario forecasts. You heard it here first.

Market timing is discussed in detail with market cycles, as well as by calendar such as the Presidential Cycle, the strategy 'Sell in May and Go Away', best and worst times to invest, etc.

The lessons from my bad experiences could be more valuable than the good ones. I achieved a huge return in 2009 in my largest taxable account and revealed my secrets here. The bottom fishing strategy could be the most profitable during the early market recovery, but we need to discover when exactly that recovery occurs.

This book is intended for someone with more knowledge than the beginner retail investor. It is part of the series "Tools in Investing", which should cover most topics in investing.

How this book is organized

This book has 7 sections (6 sections plus the bonus section) covering most areas in market timing from my personal experience.

Most graphs and tables are in landscape orientation for both paperback and e-readers. Some graphs may not be displayed adequately on a small screen of an e-reader. E-readers may be available in the current version of Windows, so you can read e-books on the larger screen of your PC. For better orientation, just flip the e-readers 90 degrees.

A link is usually included for these screens. Copy it to your browser to display the graphs on your PC if desirable. Instructions on how to produce some graphs are provided as you should try them out. One example is how to produce a chart on detecting market crashes.

It is easier to display some tables in landscape mode. Select a table or a graph via your e-reader to display it to fit the screen.

The font size and page size of most e-book formats can be adjusted. The unknown, special character is the "smiling face" that the current Kindle does not convert correctly as of this writing.

There are clickable links to web articles. Most of them are from my own websites and public websites such as Wikipedia. Some public links may not be available in the future as they are not under my control and my book offerings may change.

Fidelity Video provides video clips to explain some basic terms and it may require Fidelity customers to sign on in order to view them. Check the trial offer from Fidelity. YouTube offers similar video lessons.

These links extend the usefulness of this book by making available specific topics that may not be interesting to every reader. It also provides articles (most are not written by me) for more in-depth analyzes.

The current version provides most of the links the paperback readers can enter into your browser. Get the same information by entering a search in Wikipedia such as Dogs of Dow.

Investopedia is another source beside Wikipedia.
http://www.investopedia.com/

'Afterthoughts' includes my additional comments and comments from others. Readers can make comments in this book's website. These comments may be included in the Afterthoughts in subsequent revisions, with the commenter's last name redacted. It is the section of the article for freer and informal discussion. It also contains some political and social issues.

There are fillers with tips and jokes (most original) to fill up the empty space of the printed book. Fillers, links and afterthoughts may disrupt the flow of reading this book. However, no readers so far ask me to take them out.

For convenience, this book uses SPY, an Exchange Traded Fund (ETF) simulating the S&P 500, as the benchmark for the market.

Annualized returns (Return * 365 / (Days between)) are used where appropriate for more meaningful comparison. To illustrate, I have a 10% return in 6 months, a 10% in a year and a 10% in 2 years. It is more meaningful to use annualized returns of 20%, 10% and 5% respectively for the 6-month return, the one-year return and the 2-year return in this example.

Usually I do not include the dividend, so you can add an estimated 1.5% to the annualized return. In addition, compound interest is not used for easier calculation, so the actual return could be even better.

About the author
I graduated from Cal. State University at San Jose in Industrial Engineering and University of Mass. in Amherst with a MS in Industrial Engineering. My articles in SeekingAlpha.com.
Click the link (http://seekingalpha.com/author/tony-pow/articles) and this recent article.

Dedication
To all retail investors and future retail investors including my grandchildren. I sincerely hope this book will build bridges with fellow investors with different backgrounds.

Acknowledgement
Thanks to all the free websites that make this book more useful.

Important notices

This book is based on my older book Market timing which was published in 11/2013.

Version	Paperback	e-Book
1.0	02/16	02/16
2.0	11/19	11/19
2.4	05/22	05/22
2.6		05/25

Book store managers can order the paper version of this book from Createspace.com.
https://tonyp4idea.blogspot.com/2020/12/book-managers.html
Book update.
https://ebmyth.blogspot.com/2020/12/updates-for-all-books.html

Disclaimer

parameters such as RSI(14) are arbitrarily set by me. I have made a lot of predictions that may not materialize. My publisher and I are not liable for any damages in using this book or its contents.

How the rate of return is calculated

They are for education purposes only, and do not make your investing decisions based on them. I usually use annualized for better comparisons; 4% in a month is more than 5% in a year for example. For short-term strategies including momentum, shorting and year-end strategy, I use the returns for a month, and sometimes including returns for 2 months for comparison. Annualized returns are usually used for long-term strategies. The holding periods may have a few days off due to holidays and weekends. For simplicity, most of my returns do not include commissions, exchange fees, order spread and dividends. Most numbers have been rounded up for better readability. The return = profit / investment. I and my publisher are not liable for any error. I use SPY and sometimes RSP as a yardstick; RSP and SPY have the same S&P 500 stocks, but the stocks are weighted evenly in RSP. However, many readers do not know RSP.

*** Market Timing

Overview

Market timing is a strategy that involves making educated guesses about future market movements to reduce risk and maximize financial gains. While the market generally trends upward over long periods, short-term fluctuations can result in significant losses during market downturns. Understanding these trends and acting accordingly can protect and grow your investment portfolio.

Between 2000 and 2014, the market experienced two significant crashes with losses averaging around 45%. Bull markets tend to last over 10 years, while bear markets generally last less than two years. Successfully timing the market could yield an average annual return of around 10% during bull markets, but failure to act during bear markets may lead to losses of around 40%.

The Concept of Market Timing

Market timing can be compared to harvesting apples. Just like picking apples at the right time yields the best fruit, investing at the right time yields the highest returns. However, market timing is based on informed guesses and involves risk. A proven system with general guidelines can minimize potential losses and enhance long-term gains.

Market Timing Categories

Market timing can be categorized based on duration as follows:
1. **Secular Cycle (20 years)** - Long-term market trends often spanning decades.
2. **Market Cycle (5 years)** - Periods of sustained market growth or decline.
3. **Correction (10-20%)** - Minor market pullbacks occurring once or twice a year.

Market plunges with losses between 30% to 55% are usually rapid. The methods outlined here aim to reduce losses by signaling when to exit and re-enter the market. Although they may not precisely identify market peaks or bottoms, they significantly reduce losses.

Current Market Trends

Each market has unique conditions. For instance, excessive money printing in recent years has altered traditional market cycle lengths. If the U.S. dollar loses its reserve currency status, market behavior will shift, and historical market principles may no longer apply.

Actions to Take

Predicting the market with absolute certainty is impossible. However, being proactive can safeguard investments. Consider the following strategies:

1. **Move to Cash** - Shift risky investments to cash during market downturns. This reduces potential losses but may incur tax consequences in non-retirement accounts.
2. **Diversify** - Spread investments across lower-risk assets such as bonds and CDs. The proportion depends on your risk tolerance.
3. **Set Stop Orders** - Use trailing stop orders to automatically sell investments if their value drops below a set threshold. Manual stop orders can help avoid market manipulation.

Analysis: Fundamental vs Technical

Fundamental analysis evaluates whether the market is overvalued based on financial metrics such as Price-to-Earnings (P/E) ratio, debt-to-GDP ratio, and overall economic health. Technical analysis monitors market trends through price movements and technical indicators such as SMA-50, SMA-200, and RSI.

Key Market Indicators

1. **Technical Indicators**
   - **Death Cross**: A bearish signal when the 50-day moving average crosses below the 200-day moving average.
   - **SMA-350**: Price trading above the 350-day moving average suggests a healthy market.
   - **RSI (Relative Strength Index)**: An RSI below 70 indicates no overbuying.

2. **Fundamental Indicators**
   - **P/E Ratio**: A high ratio signals overvaluation.
   - **Debt-to-GDP**: A high ratio indicates economic strain.

    o **Flow to Equity/Bond**: Tracks movement of investments between stocks and bonds.

Current Market Outlook

As of 2021, the market has been technically sound but fundamentally unsound. Excessive money printing, high corporate debt, and political uncertainties have raised risks. Following technical indicators for entry and exit points can mitigate losses. There are many case studies after 2021.

Final Thoughts

The market is unpredictable, but using a structured market timing approach can minimize losses and maximize gains. Continue monitoring economic trends, adjust strategies accordingly, and prioritize capital preservation. Regularly review market conditions to make informed investment decisions. My experience indicates technical analysis is more important than fundamental analysis.

1   Ask AI (ChatGPT) for 2025 Outlook

This is a practical query of the previous article. Ask "The probability of a market crash" on 1/2025. Try it as the current market could indicate otherwise. However, most likely their data bases have **not been outdated.** Most factors have been described in this book. The following is displayed on with my comments. Compare this article with the Overview if time permits.

The chance of a market crash depends on various factors, including economic indicators, geopolitical events, monetary policies, and investor sentiment. While predicting the exact timing of a crash is impossible, several signals can indicate heightened risks. Here's an overview of factors that can increase the likelihood of a market downturn:

Comment. Technical Analysis is more important than fundamental analysis in market timing. I prefer my version of Death Cross for no chart and SMA-350 (when SPY dips below the SMA-350 line)

Key Risk Indicators for a Market Crash
    1. **Economic Slowdown or Recession**:

- o Declining GDP growth, rising unemployment, or reduced consumer spending are warning signs.
- o If inflation outpaces wages, consumer demand may decline, leading to a slowdown.

2. **High Valuations**:
   - o When stock valuations (e.g., Price-to-Earnings ratios) are far above historical averages, it signals a potential bubble. For example, the tech sector in 2000 or housing in 2007.

3. **Rising Interest Rates**:
   - o The Federal Reserve (or other central banks) raising interest rates to combat inflation can hurt growth, increase borrowing costs, and weigh on company profits.
   - o This often results in capital flowing out of equities and into bonds.

4. **Excessive Market Leverage**:
   - o High margin debt or leveraged bets often precede crashes, as forced selling can trigger rapid declines during corrections.

5. **Geopolitical Tensions**:
   - o Events like wars, trade conflicts, or major political instability (e.g., U.S.-China relations or the Ukraine war) can rattle markets.

6. **Corporate Earnings Decline**:
   - o A sustained decline in corporate profitability reduces investor confidence, particularly in high-growth sectors.

7. **Overdependence on Stimulus**:
   - o Post-COVID-19 market growth was partly driven by fiscal stimulus and low interest rates. A withdrawal of liquidity from the market ("quantitative tightening") could lead to corrections.

8. **Sectoral or Asset-Specific Bubbles**:
   - o Overheated sectors, such as tech stocks (e.g., FAANG), cryptocurrencies, or real estate, could drag down broader indices if bubbles burst.

9. **Market Psychology**:
   - o Fear-driven selling often exacerbates downturns. This can be triggered by events such as a high-

profile corporate failure, surprising inflation reports, or aggressive Federal Reserve actions.

Likelihood of a Market Crash in 2025

Current trends (as of early 2025) influencing crash probabilities include:

- **Persistent Inflation or Deflation Risks**: If central banks tighten policy too aggressively or fail to manage inflation, growth could stall.
- **High Debt Levels**: Both government and corporate debt remain high, making markets more vulnerable to shocks.
- **AI and Tech Volatility**: Overvaluation in emerging technologies (like AI) may pose risks if optimism fades.

However, it's essential to note that:

- Most crashes are preceded by years of warning signals.
- Markets tend to rebound over time after downturns, which underscores the importance of long-term investing.

Comment. AI usually does not give you exact numbers. You can search them from many sources. Fidelity's Viewpoint (register required) usually have good insights.

How to Prepare for a Potential Crash

1. **Diversify Investments**:
   - Spread your portfolio across sectors, regions, and asset classes (e.g., bonds, commodities, real estate).

   Comment. Gold (GLD for ETF) and silver (SLV for ETF).
2. **Focus on Quality Assets**:
   - Invest in companies with strong balance sheets, consistent earnings, and low debt.
3. **Consider Defensive Sectors**:
   - Healthcare, utilities, and consumer staples often perform better during downturns.
4. **Use Stop-Loss Orders**:
   - Set automatic sell orders to limit losses on individual stocks.
5. **Maintain Cash Reserves**:
   - Having liquidity lets you capitalize on opportunities during corrections.

> **Comment.** Aggressive investors can buy contra ETFs (betting the market going down further), and even shorting stocks (for taxable accounts).

6. **Monitor Indicators**:
   o Keep an eye on key metrics like the yield curve, corporate earnings, and market sentiment.
7. **Avoid Panic Selling**:
   o Market downturns are often temporary. History shows that markets recover, sometimes within a few years.

Comment. Return to equity when the market recovers. They are among my best years in investing.

As of Jan., 2025, the market is tough to predict. Several major investors including Buffett is accumulating cash, while many fund managers predict a bull market for the year. The market is making new heights in January.

I choose the middle ground. Usually, I sell 2 stocks and buy one. At the end of January, I have about 10% in cash, CDs and some contra ETFs from my rough estimate. I watch technical indicators more frequently.

Fidelity's prediction (Insight)

Click on "News & Research" and then "Stock Market & Sector Performance" and "Market") for Equity Market Commentary. The advantage is that Fidelity does not require paid subscriptions to see the entire article.

Ask AI on the current market direction

2   More notes on market timing

Cycles and corrections

I divide the market timing in three categories by durations as follows. All time durations are estimates for discussion and all markets are different

	Duration
Secular cycle	20 years (actually less)
Market Cycle	5 years (not the current one)
Correction: 10-20%	1 per year
5-10%	2 per year (count the above as 1)

Market plunges have losses between 30% and 55% usually. There is a gray area for the 20% to 30% losses, which does not happen often. When the market plunges, it plunges hard and fast. The techniques in this book tell you to exit the market and when to return to equities. The techniques are based on falling prices, so they will not indicate peaks and bottoms, but they will help you to reduce further losses.

Within the secular market, there are market cycles. There is a super cycle that I ignore as I find it not too useful. Every market is different. Today we have excessive money printing that changes all the previous logic such as the average length of a market cycle. If the USD is not the reserved currency, the market would fall. However, the correlation of the market and the economy will correlate again. We do not know when, but it will. Otherwise, we have to rewrite all the books on investing.

For instant gratification, you can read Simplest Way to Time the Market and skip the rest of this lengthy section for now.

Canary warning?
When I was working on my new book "Best stocks to buy for 2021" on Dec. 10, 2020, I found something really strange. I have never rejected so many stocks that have Fidelity's Equity Summary Score higher than 9. I rejected them as there was a lot of dumping from the insiders. Insiders know their companies better than most of us. Is it the canary telling us the market is overvalued?

Initially the following stocks have been screened by my value screens. Buy any one of the following stocks, only if you have good reason(s). How can HEAR score a perfect 10 while the Insiders' Transaction is -75% (to me -2% is normal). The analysts must be wrong this time, or they believe the market will continuously make new heights.

Symbol	Fidelity Score	Insider Purchase	Return[1]	Annualized
BCC	9.9	-24%	46%	126%
GPI	10.0	-17%	35%	95%
HEAR	10.0	-75%	43%	118%
HVT	9.5	-37%	53%	144%
HZO	9.5	-27%	75%	204%
Average				84%
SPY				30%
Beat SPY[2]				177%

[1] From Dec. 20, 2020 to July 1, 2021. Fees, commissions and dividends are not included.

[2] = (Average – SPY) /SPY. SPY represents the market to many of us. This concludes the Insiders are wrong in this case.

A correction or a crash?
Back in December 2018, the S&P 500 had dropped around 15%. That qualifies as a **correction**. A true **crash** would have required an additional 30% drop—around a 45% total loss.

The real question: **Was that the bottom, or is there more to come?** Are we looking at genuine bargains—or just a trap? That's the trillion-dollar question.

Major crashes usually have identifiable **triggers**, like the 2008 financial crisis or the 2000 dot-com bubble. As of late 2018, aside from record-high **margin debt**, potential **Trump impeachment**, or a **trade war**, I didn't see an obvious catalyst.

Links
Search articles from Google and YouTube on today's market conditions.
YouTube: 1
https://www.youtube.com/watch?v=czHUI0syjKo&t=300s

Section I: Spotting big market plunges

1 Spotting big market plunges

This chapter is longer and conceptually dense. You'll get the best results by applying these ideas yourself. The payoff, however, can be substantial. No single method can predict market cycles perfectly, but combining the following hints increases your odds of making better decisions. The **first hint—Technical Analysis—is the most important**.

No one can consistently call every market top or bottom. This chapter is for educational purposes. But if our guesses are more right than wrong over time, we'll do well. As with everything in investing, **there are no guarantees**.

Market plunges, defined here as losses of **30% to 55% from top to bottom**, can erase most gains of an entire cycle. Our goal is to **avoid at least half the loss**. Avoid buying stocks during these plunges, which often last more than a year—from market peak to market bottom. For many investors, the decision to exit or stay in is worth millions. The methods here aren't foolproof, but they've worked well for me in past cycles.

Between 2000 and 2008, my **SMA-350** strategy produced only one false signal out of three. Since then, volatility has increased, resulting in more false alarms. To manage this, **don't move all your assets to cash at once**. Adjust based on your risk tolerance. Often, the market gives a quick reentry signal, minimizing missed gains. Just be aware of potential tax consequences in taxable accounts.

Eleven Hints to Spot a Market Plunge

1. Technical Analysis (TA) — The Most Important Indicator

Use the **350-day Simple Moving Average (SMA-350)**. If prices fall below this line, it's a warning. When prices rise back above it, it may signal recovery. This method caught both the 2000 and 2008 plunges early enough to act.

The following chart is created by Yahoo!Finance. If it does not display well on a small screen, copy the following link to your browser to display it on your PC.
http://ebmyth.blogspot.com/2013/05/ta-graph-for-spotting-plunges-chapter.html

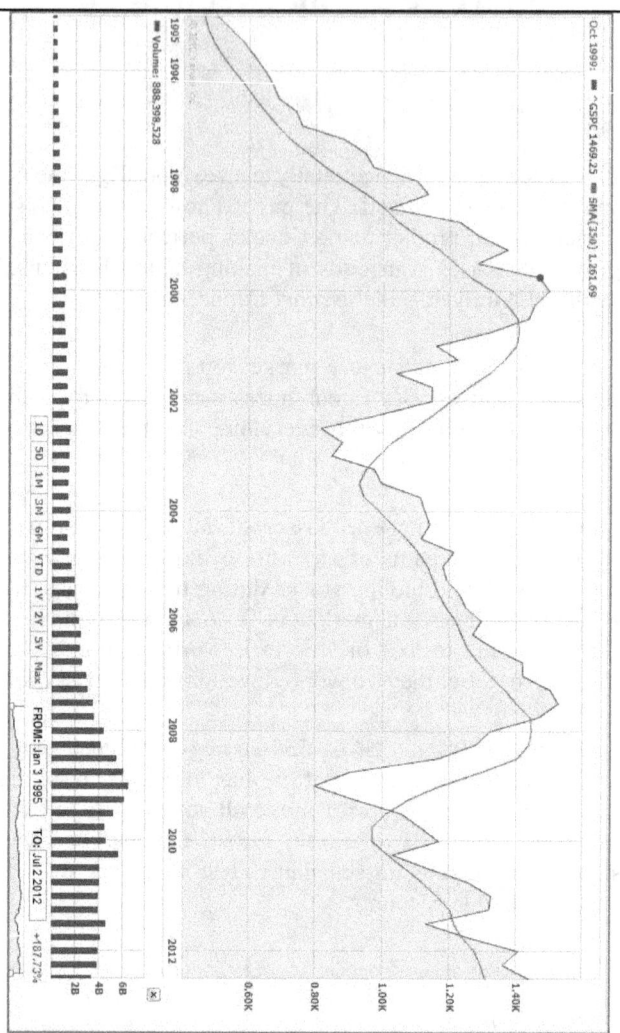

350 days simple moving average (SMA). Yahoo!Finance

Example:

- **Exit**: Q1 2000 | **Re-enter**: Q1 2003
- **Exit**: Dec. 2008 | **Re-enter**: July 2009

While no indicator is perfect, the SMA-350 often limits large losses. Think of it like insurance—it may cost you some gains, but can protect you when it matters most.

To create the chart:

- Use Yahoo! Finance, Fidelity, or StockCharts.com.
- Enter SPY or QQQ (for tech-heavy portfolios).
- Add a **350-day SMA** (or ~11.67 months).
- Zoom in on periods like 2000 or 2008 to see the signals in action.

Note: I now use **Fidelity** for charting as Yahoo! sometimes has limitations.

2. Follow the Flow of Money

Extreme bullish behavior is a warning. When everyone claims to be a genius investor and IPOs are booming without profit, it's time to be cautious. In 1999, dot-com companies handed out cash just for signing up. Their business plans were laughable, yet valuations soared.

Watch **AAII bullish sentiment**—if it crosses 70%, consider it a red flag. Rising equity inflows and retail frenzy are also strong contrarian indicators.

3. Market Cycle Duration

Market cycles typically last **4 to 5 years**, but this varies. As of late 2018, we were in one of the longest bull markets on record. The longer the peak, the greater the risk of a steep drop. I call this **Newton's Law of Investing**: what goes up must eventually come down.

4. Valuation Metrics

Use historical **P/E ratios** as a guide:

- S&P 500 average P/E ≈ 15–16.5
- A sector P/E above **35** often signals a coming correction
- A sector P/E above **40** suggests a market peak

For example:

- P/E was 28 in 2000, 18 in 2007, and 16 in 2015—all above average.
  Note that today's valuations are influenced by low borrowing costs and globalization. Always adjust expectations to the current macro context.

5. Bubble Triggers

Past bubbles were easy to see in hindsight:

- **2000**: Tech bubble
- **2007**: Housing/mortgage bubble

I shifted to traditional sectors in early April 2000—barely ahead of the crash. I did well in oil in 2007 but took losses in 2008 across the board. Following these hints back then would've saved me a lot.

6. Rising Interest Rates

Higher interest rates:

- Increase borrowing costs
- Reduce consumer spending
- Raise the cost of margin

Watch for spikes in **margin debt** and **Fed discount rates above 5%**. These usually precede a downturn. Conversely, a **rate below 1%** may mark a market bottom—time to consider re-entering equities.

7. Yield Curve Inversion

When **short-term yields exceed long-term yields**, recession often follows. A common signal is when the **2-year yield > 10-year yield**.

As of Oct. 15, 2018, yields were nearly equal—suggesting caution. Historically, this indicator has only had **two false positives** out of seven recessions.

8. Oil Price Fluctuations

Extreme oil prices are destabilizing:

- **Above $120** or **below $30** = caution
- Falling oil prices can indicate global economic stress

In 2015–2016, oil price collapses forced oil-rich nations to liquidate equities, dragging markets down with them.

9. Expert Opinions

Ignore loud media voices and sales pitches. Instead, follow thoughtful commentary. In 2000, an article comparing a hyped startup's market cap to a real company's conference room size helped me exit tech.

Good insights, when planted in a well-prepared mind, yield results.

10. Political and Economic Policies

Markets rose from 2009–2016 largely due to **low interest rates**, not strong economic performance. Fed policy is key. Political decisions like **Trump's proposed tariffs** in 2016 posed global recession risks.

Pay attention to macroeconomic levers.

11. Miscellaneous Signals

- In 2000, an article about overhyped companies helped me exit.
- In 2008, a **"Double Top"** technical pattern signaled a major downturn.

Be Conservative

Start small. Don't risk your entire portfolio based on new strategies— especially from a book you paid $25 for. Think of early exits as **cheap insurance**—you might lose small gains, but avoid catastrophic losses.

The **SMA-350** worked well for both 2000 and 2008. That said:

- Future crashes may unfold faster.
- Popular strategies may lose edge if widely adopted.
- The market is rarely rational.
- Since 2011, we've seen more noise (false signals).
- Adjust your strategy to your risk tolerance.

For less noise, use **longer SMAs (like 400 days)**. Shorter ones (like 200) are more sensitive but prone to false alarms.

Conclusion

This chapter shares my practical tools and insights into market timing. Markets aren't always rational. If they were, everyone would be rich. When you sense risk, **check the charts more often** and read what credible market experts are saying.

Market timing isn't an exact science—it's educated guessing. With enough experience and discipline, your guesses can tilt the odds in your favor. **Technical analysis (especially SMA-350)** often beats "Buy and Hold" during major downturns. But always respect your risk tolerance and use strategies you understand.

Links:
Market crash
https://www.youtube.com/watch?v=GJD2BYhVyrM
6 Signs of market crash
https://www.youtube.com/watch?v=ynCXHgeZ_K8

2   More tools

Using VIX as a timing model

When I overlapped VIX and the S&P 500 index, I found a consistent pattern. However, it has not been conclusive to me. Try to enter VIX in any chart system such as Yahoo!Finance with the S&P 500 overlaid. In the summer of 2008, VIX jumped about 500% from about 15 to 89.

VIX
http://en.wikipedia.org/wiki/VIX
VIX from Yahoo!Finance.
http://finance.yahoo.com/echarts?s=^VIX+Interactive#
There are several articles on the topic.
http://seekingalpha.com/instablog/434935-south-gent/3373095-vix-asset-allocation-model.
Ted Talk: 1
http://www.ted.com/talks/didier_sornette_how_we_can_predict_the_next_financial_crisis

Other technical indicators

- Head and Shoulder would predict a market plunge as evidenced in 2007. The reverse pattern would predict a market surge as indicated in 2009.
- Double Top is a bearish signal and double bottom is a bullish signal.
- Death Cross is used to detect large plunges and it does not require charting via Finviz.com. Golden Cross detects when to return.
- MACD (Moving Average Convergence Divergence). When the indicator is below the zero line, it is bearish and vice versa. Use it as a secondary indicator to detect the market direction.
- When RSI (14) is over 65%, the market is most likely overbought (i.e., overvalued).
- Use the following SMA-20 as a secondary indicator as an alternative to the SMA-350. When the stock price is below SMA-20 (Single Moving Average for the last 20 sessions) for three consecutive days, it indicates a possible market plunge. In theory, the institutional investors dump the stock on the first day and then the retail investors follow on the second day. If it

continues on the third day, most likely it is not the trick of the institutional investors to take advantage of the retail investors.

Sound Advice Risk Indicator

We only invest in stocks or real estates in a crude sense. This indicator comparing the allocations between these two investments has been quite successful. When we invest too much in the stock market instead of real estate, we will expect a market crash. When this index hit 2 as in 1906, 1928, 1937 and 1965, we had market crashes at all these times. Today (12/2018), we have a similar warning. Use Google to search for articles mentioning this indicator. Here is one of many.

Buffett's Equity to GDP

It measures the value of the market. It has been quite successful. Google for the current value. Advisor Perspectives may have this value and many insights on the current market. It will not detect the peaks and bottoms as no one can consistently. About a third of the earnings of the S&P 500 companies come from abroad. Hence it boosts market cap but doesn't include those countries' GDP. This is a major fault.

https://www.youtube.com/watch?v=dexOhg3pYa0

3   Related topics

Other related hints on value

The oil and industrial commodities (copper, steel...) are within 20% of their record highs. From my memory, it is the first time that oil is in sync with the market due to the dumping of stocks by the oil-producing countries today.

The total market cap is higher than the GDP. As of Nov., 2013, "Market Cap / GDP" is about 110% (fair value at 85%) and hence it is overvalued. Daily ratios can be obtained from GuruFocus.com, a paid subscription service. It does not work in the current cycle from 2008. It may be today because most large companies are multinational. However, today most large companies are global companies, so it loses some luster in using this ratio.

Dow Theory and many similar market timing strategies may become less effective as every market is different. Many ignore the service industries such as selling music and games via downloading.

From my observation, the higher the interest rates are, the higher the chance that a market plunge will be. The companies will have less earnings due to the higher borrowing costs especially in businesses that require a lot of borrowing and/or most of their customers' purchases are via financing. The stocks are more expensive to buy using margin accounts. Hence, the market will not fare well when the Fed hikes the interest rate.

Q including intangible assets is with P/E in evaluating the value of the market. It is harder to calculate.

Shiller P/E (same as CAPE or PE10)

It can be used to detect the valuation of the market. The P is the S&P 500 (or use SPY) and E is the average earnings of the last 10 years. It can also be used on sector ETFs and stocks. Use it as one of the hints. The major flaw is 10 years is too long of a time.

To simplify, most likely the market valuation is low (good to buy) when the P/E is below 15. The market valuation is high when it is above 20. As of 2014, it is far above 20 (17 in 2/2016). CAPE (cyclically adjusted price/earnings ratio) is available from the web by searching "CAPE P/E" to get the current reading.

Shiller's P/E http://www.gurufocus.com/shiller-PE.php
From the above links, CAPE has been pretty decent. The reason why it does not work in 2014 is the excessive money printing that makes the market not act rationally. Treat it as a secondary yardstick at best. Here is a good article on P/E and PE10.
https://www.advisorperspectives.com/dshort/updates/2016/11/01/is-the-stock-market-cheap

He has been wrong since 2011 for calling recession every year. Here is his 2020 prediction. A bestseller has been preaching similar ideas of bubbles since 2009.

Fear and Greed

This index from cnnFn.com is a similar contrary index. Leave the market when Greed is high and vice versa.

Many high-flying internet stocks lost more than 95% of their peak values. As in any bubble, the last ones to get into the bubble suffer most. The investors make out pretty nicely if they use the strategies below:

- Use a stop loss to protect your profits. Periodically adjust the order when the stock appreciates.
- Use SMA-20 (from Finviz.com). When the stock falls below the Simple Moving Average for the last 20 sessions, sell it. Use SMA-50 instead if you have a higher risk tolerance.

Lazy man's market timing

Sound Advice Risk Indicator, Equality to GDP, Inverted Interest Curve and Death Cross make up the lazy man's market timing. Google for the current values of the four. If you cannot get the last one, calculate it from Finviz.com. The easiest is asking AI (artificial intelligence).

Fear of recession: https://www.youtube.com/watch?v=g_LeWSl2nJc

Using Fidelity Resources

To access market insights from Fidelity:
- Go to Fidelity.com
- Click "News & Research"
- Click "Stocks, ETFs and Crypto"
- Switch to "ETF" (the default is "Stock".

My Experiences with Market Timing

I didn't take market timing seriously until 2008. Here's a summary of my key decisions—some good, some lessons learned:

- **2000 – Exit:**
  After reading multiple articles about the overvaluation of internet stocks, I moved most of my sector funds—mainly tech—into more traditional sectors. In hindsight, moving to **cash** would have been more profitable. At that time, contra ETFs were not available, I couldn't short stocks in retirement accounts, and I had no experience with options.

- **2003 – Return:**
  I bet the market would recover within two years. I bought stocks with strong cash positions that could survive a prolonged downturn. I got lucky—the market rebounded that same year. One of those stocks was acquired by IBM, delivering a sizable gain.

- **2008 – Exit:**
  Although I had developed the SMA chart strategy, I ignored it. My prior success in energy stocks during 2007 gave me a false sense of security. When the crash came, energy stocks fell hard too. I sold during the crash, which was painful. In hindsight, I should have bought **contra ETFs**.

- **2009 – Return:**
  My chart gave a strong buy signal in mid-March 2009. I started buying in **February**, slightly ahead of the signal. With accumulated short-term capital losses, I actively traded to take advantage of volatility. I used a home equity loan—at a lower interest rate than my margin account—for short-term liquidity, although this is **not recommended**. I only used margin briefly between trades. That year turned out to be one of my best—I made **about 80% profit** in my largest taxable account.

About False alarms

- Between **2000 and 2010**, the SMA-350 strategy generated only **one false alarm**.
- From **2011 to 2016**, there were **more false signals** due to increased market noise and volatility.
- To reduce false alarms, you can **adjust the moving average from SMA-350 to SMA-400**. This may delay signals slightly, but helps avoid overreacting to short-term fluctuations.

Note: I generally ignore market data **prior to 2000**, as market behavior and structure have changed significantly in the modern era.

A faster, confirming indicator

In case you do not exit the market on the first sign, another faster technical indicator (SMA-50) would confirm the market plunge when it crosses over the SMA-350 downwards on Jan. 18, 2008 as an indicator in the following graph. The reentry using cross-over does not fare that well as expected.

In addition, high volume (compared to the average volume is a confirmation. To illustrate, if today's volume of SPY doubles its average daily volume, then it is a good confirmation.

Link
Double Tops:
http://www.investopedia.com/terms/d/doubletop.asp
Double Tops Video.
https://www.YouTube.com/watch?v=b-PaSDJiG2U

#Filler: Illogical English

Ever wonder why we say "I'm flying *on* a jet plane"? Realistically, only an action hero—or perhaps an unfortunate Afghan refugee— might ride *on* the outside of a plane, which makes the phrase a bit absurd (albeit darkly humorous). Shouldn't it be "in" a jet plane instead? Did Peter, Paul and Mary just go with the rhyme over logic?

4   Why the market fluctuates

The following chart uses SPY (simulating the market) with SMA-350 for the year of 2020 using Fidelity's charting function. It will be used to demonstrate how SMA-350 worked for 2020; the dates may be several days off. This article is written on 1/1/2021.

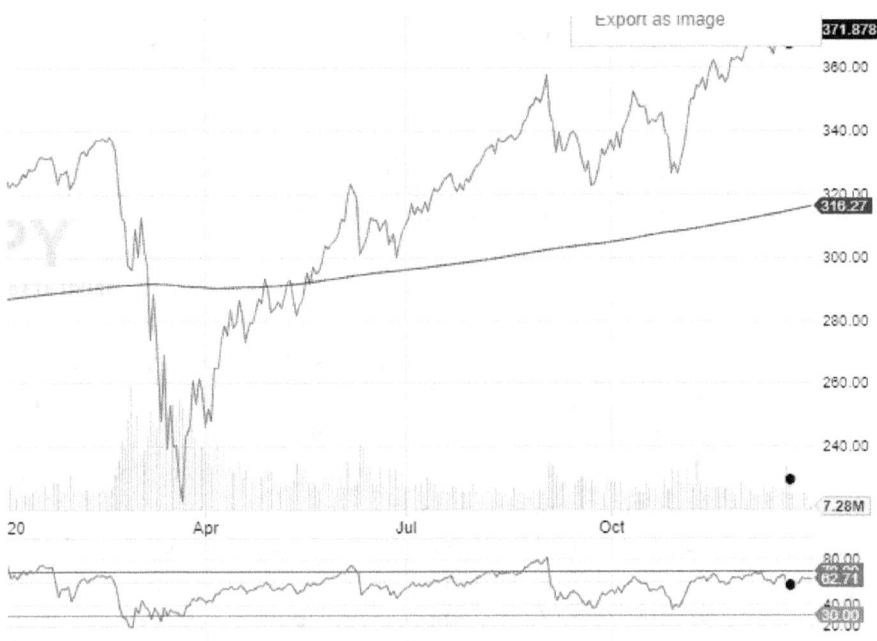

Market Timing

SMA-350 (Simple Moving Average for the last 350 sessions), described in this book, worked fine in 2020. It told us to exit the market on about 3/11/2020 and return on about the beginning of June. There were two false signals (on about 4/28 and 5/8) that told you to exit but return to the market shortly.

The other indicators are RSI(14) and P/E. Fidelity's chart uses 80 for overbought and 30 for under-bought for RSI(14). The market has been overpriced for a long while. In this case, technical analysis (SMA-350 I used in my example) works better than fundamental (P/E as one of the metrics); It has been sold for the entire 2020.

Why there is a big drop in late March and why it comes back

The trigger is the pandemic.

The market came back for many reasons:
- We understood the pandemic better.
- A lot of money on the sideline.
- The government supplies more money by printing it excessively.

- The government lowers the interest rate (almost to zero).

2021 prediction

It is quite hard to predict the market. Here are my thoughts. The market is not rational (fundamentally speaking).

For:

- The government keeps on excessively supplying money.
- With easy credit, the rising housing market leads to many profitable sectors such as furniture.
- Due to easy credit and recovery, many companies buy back their own stocks.
- Low margin interest rate usually boosts the stock market.
- If the vaccines can control this pandemic, many sectors will recover. As I demonstrated before, we have to wait one more year for some sectors such as airlines, restaurants and cruise lines.
- Trade war with China could be reduced under Biden.

Against:
- The pandemic has not been stopped.
- Unemployment is breaking the previous record.
- Small businesses continue to go bankrupt.
- Complete decoupling with China.
- The government tools do not work anymore such as lowering interest rate.
- Super inflation is due to ample supply of money chasing a fixed amount of assets (stocks for example). It would also shake the status of the USD as a reserve currency.

As in any market, there are two camps opposite to each other. Need to watch the market like a hawk and take actions accordingly (talk to your financial advisor first). I expect the plunge would cause the market to lose about 40% if it happens.

5   Double tops & a faster indicator

The following is the chart to use <u>double tops</u> to detect the last market peak in 2007.

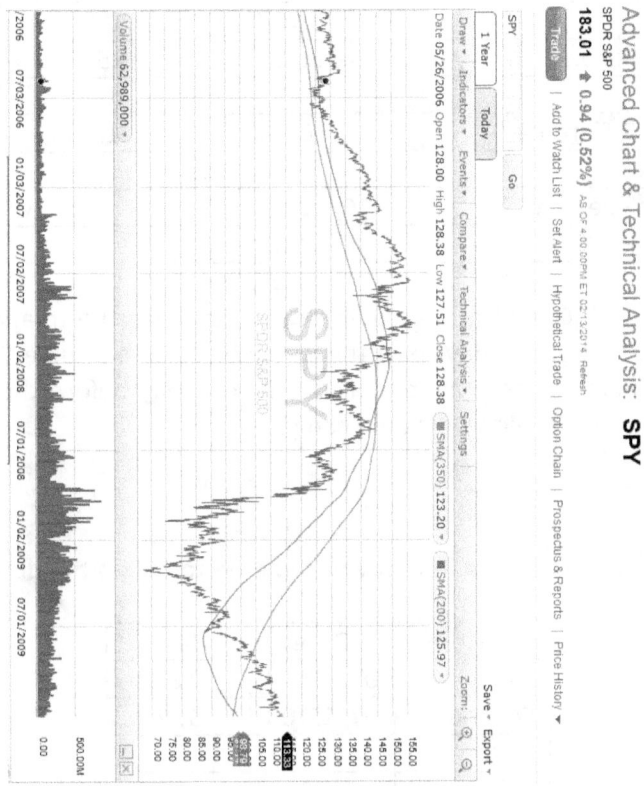

SPY: SMA.   Source: Fidelity

If you have a small screen on your e-reader, produce a similar graph using Yahoo!Finance. Enter SPY and select Technical Indicator. Select SMA and 350 days. Select the date from 1/3/2006 to 1/3/2010. Do another graph with SMA-200 as an overlay.

Critical dates

Table: Vital Dates

Market Plunge	Peak	Bottom	Indicator Exit	Indicator Reenter

| 2007 | 10/12/07 | 03/06/09 | 01/03/08 | 09/08/09 |

The following were obtained from my naked eyes to obtain the data from the graph. They are not accurate but are fine for discussion.

Top	Date	SPY
First	07/17/07	155
Second	10/11/07	157
Difference	86	1%
Selected	10/11/07	
Peak	10/12/07	

The SMA-350 indicator suggested us to exit the market on 01/03/08, about 83 days past the peak (10/12/07). Double Top is a better indicator here as it told us only one day before the peak. Will it happen again? Only time can tell.

Double Bottom

Again, the following is from my naked eyes to obtain the data from the graph.

Bottom	Date	SPY
First	03/17/08	127
Second	07/15/08	122
Difference	120	-4%
Selected	07/15/08	
Bottom	03/06/09	

Arbitrarily, I use the absolute difference of 5% or less to determine the double bottom condition (the absolute % of the second bottom to the first bottom).

The SMA-350 indicator suggests us to reenter the market on 09/08/09, about 186 days past the bottom (03/06/09). Double Bottom tells us to reenter the market about 234 days after the bottom. Hence, double bottom as defined here is not a good indicator.

It is interesting that the difference of days is 120. If we use 100 days as the threshold, then it is not qualified to be a double bottom.

We may want to use the earlier of either the chart or the double bottom to determine when to reenter the market.

Is SMA-350 better than SMA-200?
From the graph in this article, I conclude that SMA-200 has more noise that tells you to exit and reenter (or the other way) more often than SMA-350. It is logical as SMA-350 uses a longer duration (350 days vs. 200 days) for the moving average.

However, SMA-200 tells you to reenter the market earlier from the actual bottom in my limited tests. Hence, it is more profitable at least for the market plunge in 2007. For the next plunge, I would use SMA-350 to exit the market and SMA-200 to reenter the market. Is it just coincidental?

6   Retail investors and market timing

The average retail investor actually holds several **advantages over fund managers**—they have no mandates, can act quickly, and don't report to clients. Yet, paradoxically, the average retail investor **underperforms the market**.

Why? It comes down to **behavior**: most retail investors buy high and sell low, driven by herd mentality, fear, and greed.

The Data Doesn't Lie
Fidelity has repeatedly shown in its quarterly summaries that many of its retail clients **move to money market funds near market bottoms** and shift back into equities when the market is near its **short-term peaks**. These behavioral patterns make money flow into equities a potential **contrarian indicator**.

Morningstar's research supports this too. From 2000 to 2010:
- **Equity funds** earned an **annualized return of 1.6%**.

- The **average investor** earned just **0.2%**—a direct result of poor timing, buying in and out at the wrong times.

From my own experience, **investor sentiment** may influence the market **in the short term**, but over the long run, fundamentals and valuation always prevail.

This explains why "**Buy and Hold**" often appears superior. Of course, the ideal is to "**Buy low, sell high**," but few manage to do that consistently. The challenge? Overcoming the natural emotions of **fear and greed**.

Who Really Beats the Market?
Most retail investors **underperform the market**, and so do many fund managers. Logically, someone must be outperforming—and those are often **institutional investors**. That's the group we aim to match, and with the right tools—like those in this book—it's possible.

Institutional investors typically **don't time the market**, which actually gives retail investors a unique advantage: we have the **flexibility to time** our entries and exits without constraints.

Words of Wisdom
Avoid reacting impulsively to financial news. Much of it is **contradictory, sensationalized, or outdated** by the time you hear it. Publications like *The Wall Street Journal* and *Barron's* offer more value than TV soundbites.
Watch this revealing interview where Jim Cramer explains how the market can be manipulated:
https://www.youtube.com/watch?v=GOS8QgAQO-k

Afterthoughts
Here are a few insightful comments that echo the retail investor dilemma:
• **Searcher wrote:**
"It seems inevitable that I buy high and sell low. I get complacent at highs and paralyzed with fear during downturns until the pain forces me to sell. Even if I get out, I might not have the courage to get back in. So I wait for confirmation... and buy at the top."

• **Clay, a 40-year investment veteran, observed:**
"Only a small percentage consistently buy low and sell high—and it's usually the same few people. Long-term investors holding quality stocks generally outperform. Traders often exit too early and reenter too late, leading to underperformance."

• **DanT, a former stock analyst, added:**
"Retail investors have more freedom than institutions, but most sabotage themselves by reacting emotionally. Even under Peter Lynch, most Magellan shareholders **lost money**—not because the fund performed poorly, but because they bought high and sold low."
He continued:
"Market timing is risky. The more confident you are in your timing 'skills,' the more dangerous it becomes. Instead, reduce risk during booms and invest more during panics. Most people can't sit on cash—it burns a hole in their pocket. But when you have dry powder and the market dips, you'll be ready."

Final Thoughts

- **Market timing can outperform Buy and Hold**, but only for those who use it skillfully and with discipline.
- For most people, a **Buy and Hold** approach with quality investments is a safer, more realistic path.
- In 2009, many retail investors moved billions into cash **at the bottom** of the market. Who bought? **Institutional investors**—and, hopefully, **you will next time.**

Links

Advantages:
http://www.tonyp4idea.blogspot.com/2011/11/no-more-investing-hero.html

Herd mentality:
http://www.tonyp4idea.blogspot.com/2011/12/fool-of-all-fools.html

Crash of 1987: https://www.youtube.com/watch?v=jLfjEMDJubg

Filler: Cocktail parties in 1999

I had a hard time convincing my friends and coworkers in 2000. How can you tell the lottery winners not to buy lottery tickets? We do have many rocket stocks today. From my books, I recommend you use trailing stops.

Section II: Market cycle

1   Market cycle

Market Cycle Overview

"Bull markets are born on pessimism, grow on skepticism, mature on optimism, and die on euphoria." – Sir John Templeton

The stock market moves in cycles, typically spanning around five years, though variations exist. These cycles can be divided into four stages: Bottom, Early Recovery, Up, and Peak. Each stage requires a tailored investment strategy to optimize returns and mitigate risks.

The Four Stages of a Market Cycle
1. Bottom
The Bottom stage follows a major market plunge, often exceeding a 25% loss within a few months. During this phase, it is prudent to refrain from investing for at least six months to a year after the initial downturn, except for aggressive investors who may consider contra ETFs or short selling.

Historically, it takes approximately a year from the plunge's onset to reach the bottom. Stocks, especially from sectors responsible for the plunge, may remain under pressure for about two years. However, high-yield corporate bonds (junk bonds) tend to perform well as interest rates are lowered to stimulate the economy.
During the 2007-2008 financial crisis, long-term bonds appreciated significantly once interest rates dropped. Proper timing of bond investments during such phases can yield substantial profits.

2. Early Recovery
The Early Recovery phase typically starts around one year after the market bottom, although pinpointing the exact moment is challenging. Investors should close out contra ETF positions and shorts during this period.

The first year of recovery often presents the most significant gains, sometimes exceeding 25%. Value stocks generally outperform growth stocks in this phase. Investors should focus on stocks with strong fundamentals and a sustainable cash reserve to weather the downturn.

During this stage, small-cap stocks with innovative technologies and solid customer bases often yield exceptional returns, especially if they become acquisition targets.

3. Up

As the market gains momentum, growth metrics like PEG (Price/Earnings to Growth) become more valuable than traditional value metrics. Most stocks, except contra ETFs and short positions, perform well.

Investors should prioritize stocks with strong growth prospects and favorable SMA-200% indicators. Although many stocks may already show significant appreciation, the "buy high, sell higher" strategy is often effective during this phase. Protecting profits with stop-loss orders is crucial.

It is advisable to avoid stocks with excessive P/E ratios (above 35) unless justified by exceptional growth potential. Additionally, be cautious of overbought stocks (RSI(14) exceeding 65) as institutional investors may trigger sharp declines.

4. Peak

The Peak phase is characterized by widespread market optimism, easy money-making, and high interest rates. It is essential to employ stop-loss and stop-limit orders to protect investments. Monitoring for potential bubbles, like the tech bubble of 2000 or the financial bubble of 2007, is crucial.

Technical analysis should be conducted regularly, and investors should prepare to shift a substantial portion of their portfolio into cash (between 25% to 50% depending on risk tolerance). Avoid becoming emotionally attached to stocks, as opportunities to repurchase at lower prices will likely arise post-plunge.

The 2007 Market Cycle Example

The market cycle from 2007 to 2016 exemplifies these stages:
- **Plunge:** October 2007 to March 2009
- **Bottom:** March 2009
- **Early Recovery:** March 2009 onwards
- **Up:** 2010 to January 2013
- **Peak:** March 2016 (as per defined market behavior)

Events and Triggers

Key economic events and government actions can influence market phases:

- Changes in interest rates
- Employment shifts
- Gross National Product (GNP) changes

While these events rarely alter the sequence of phases, they may impact their duration.

Sector Performance Across Phases

Market Phase	Favorable Sectors	Unfavorable Sectors
Early Recovery	Financial, Technology, Industrial	Energy, Telecom, Utilities
Up	Technology, Industrial, Housing	None
Peak	Mineral, Healthcare, Energy, Consumer Discretionary	Long-Term Bonds
Bottom	Consumer Staples, Utilities	Technology, Industrial, Bonds

Sectors responsible for plunges typically take longer to recover. For example, the tech sector struggled post-2000 and financials post-2007.

Conclusion

Market timing is not an exact science but making informed investment decisions based on market cycles can enhance profitability. Investors should remain vigilant, avoid emotional decisions, and be ready to shift strategies as market conditions change.

Regularly reviewing technical charts, tracking economic events, and understanding market phases are essential practices. Avoid attempting to capture the last gains of a bull market, as it often leads to significant losses during downturns.

Final Thoughts

Understanding market cycles and implementing strategic investment approaches can significantly protect and grow wealth.

Stay informed, stay adaptable, and optimize your investment decisions according to market phases.

Afterthoughts

- The Dow Theory has a lot of followers in detecting market directions. In a nutshell, the market heading upwards is confirmed by the Industrial Index and the Transportation Index (less important in today's market especially with internet sales such as songs and movies), and vice versa. As of 4/2014, the two indexes are not in uniform.
http://finance.yahoo.com/blogs/talking-numbers/this-is-a-130-year-old-warning-sign-for-stocks-231901097.html

  - The bear market has the following three phases.
  1. The market is overvalued.
  2. Corporations are not doing well with decreasing earnings and sales.
  3. Investors are selling due to fears.

  It is the reverse for a bull market: 1.The market is under-valued. 2. The market increases due to increasing corporate profits/sales and 3. Investors are buying due to greed.
- Investopedia has several articles on this topic.
http://www.investopedia.com/terms/b/businesscycle.asp
- The yield curve could predict the interest rates change and hence the economy. There are three main types of yield curve shapes: normal, flat and inverted.

  A normal yield curve is one in which longer maturity bonds have a higher yield. Similarly, the long-term CD should have a higher interest rate than the short-term CD.

  When the shorter-term yields are higher than the longer-term yields, it indicates an upcoming recession. A flat yield curve indicates the economy is transiting. Now, you've read the essence of a book on this topic costing about $50 to buy.

  However, especially today, it does not mean anything as the government supplies too much money to stimulate the economy unsuccessfully. My simple chart described using SMA-350 (Simple Moving Average for 350 trading sessions) which depends on the stock price works better. Click here for "The dynamic yield curve" (http://stockcharts.com/freecharts/yieldcurve.php).

The interest rate plays a role too. The easy money encourages folks to borrow money to buy stocks and companies to acquire other companies.

- As of Feb., 2013, I believe we're in the Up stage of the market cycle. I checked the performances of my top screens from each stage (a.k.a. phase) of the market cycle for the last 60 days. The best performance as a group belongs to the screens for the Up stage. Controversial! Always use the screens (same as searches) that perform well recently.

  In addition, the market has recovered 120% of the loss of 2007-2008. Hence the duration for an average Up stage of the market is quite close.

- Total Market Cap / GNP ratio is hotly debated on the market value. Different from the traditional 100%, I would suggest that the boundary ratio should be 130%. If it is over 130%, the market is overvalued and vice versa.
  http://www.investopedia.com/terms/m/marketcapgdp.asp
  Market cycle:
  https://www.youtube.com/watch?v=ebWL2TrIssA
  Bull market:
  https://www.investopedia.com/terms/b/bullmarket.asp

2   Bull vs. Bear market: How to navigate the cycle

Bull and Bear Market Basics
In simple terms, **most investments rise during a bull market** and fall during a bear market. These shifts are often indicated by technical signals such as the **Golden Cross** (bullish) and **Death Cross** (bearish).

The bear market in 2022 is a good example: not only did stocks fall, but **even bonds performed poorly**, mainly due to the Federal Reserve raising interest rates rapidly in response to inflation. If inflation were under control, the Fed wouldn't need to keep hiking rates.

Market and Economic Cycles

The stock market generally **leads** the economy. When interest rates are low, companies have easier access to capital, driving profits and boosting the broader economy. Eventually, the economy overheats, prompting the Fed to raise rates to prevent bubbles. As borrowing becomes costlier, businesses slow down, and layoffs begin.

To restart growth, the Fed will eventually **cut rates**, beginning a new cycle.

#Filler: Destruction of a country

Is the membership of NATO worth the destruction of a country? Definitely not. A good politician should get the membership before his announcement. Murdering citizens is a war crime to me.

2   Actions for different stages of a market cycle

There are different strategies for the different stages of the market cycle.

Strategies during market plunges

The market plunge is defined as the period between the market peak and the market bottom. It usually lasts for one year or two.

When you spot the potential plunge, consider the following actions. It depends on your risk tolerance and your investment style.

1. Contrary to popular belief, parking cash is a strategy too. Cash is needed later to move back to equities.

2. Be conservative: Buy stocks based on value and not based on momentum. Reduce your new purchases and take profits especially on momentum stocks. I buy one stock for every two or three stocks I sold during this stage.

3. Protect your portfolio with stop orders. It is one of the few times I recommend stop orders. If you watch the market every day, just place market orders when your stock falls to a specific price.

4. Buy contra ETFs for aggressive investors.

5. Sell cover calls. I prefer to sell the stocks I own.

6. Older folks may not want to sell the stocks with huge gains (due to tax consideration) or stocks that give them an income stream of dividends. They can use options to protect potential losses for the stocks they own.

What to do after the plunge

In the first year after the start of the plunge, do not start to buy unless they are very good values. Aggressive investors should start closing their short positions/put options and selling contra ETFs.

When the market plunges, it usually takes at least one year to recover as investors believe they have to sell to protect their remaining nest eggs. Those sectors that cause the bubble will take even longer to recover.

After the plunge, watch out for the interest rate. If it is still high, it is the best time to buy high-yield bonds (i.e., junk bonds). Ensure that the corporation issuing the bonds would not bankrupt; the bonds from the old GM in 2007 lost most of their values. They will appreciate when the interest rate drops that the government would routinely do to stimulate the economy. 2008 is not a good year to invest in stocks and bonds except the contra ETFs and selling shorts, but 2009 definitely is (it is my Early Recovery phase of the market cycle).

Personally, I prefer not to buy any stocks until the chart tells us to reenter the market. It is the fear that investors do not want to reenter the market. The market will always recover as in the past.

Even before the recovery, some sectors (called consumer staple) are doing better such as health care, foodstuff, utilities and pharmaceuticals that are always in demand. Interest-sensitive sectors such as housing and auto will suffer disproportionately. They are also called cyclical stocks. Consumer Discretionary are sectors that suffer a lot in a recession such as high-tech products.

What to do in early recovery and after

When the market is starting to recover (2003 and 2009 in the last two market cycles), the potential profit is the highest. Buy deeply-valued stocks on companies that have been beaten down. They will recover with the highest appreciation potential. I call it the bottom fishing strategy.

Larger companies are fishing too to acquire smaller companies that fit into their corporate synergy or small companies with the technology and/or the customer base they need.

Valued stocks could be defined a little differently in this phase. Many times P/E is not a good metric as most companies are losing money. 2003 is such a year. If you expect the recession to end in 2 years and the company has enough cash to survive in two years based on its annual burn rate, then it would be a buy candidate.

In both 2003 and 2009, I spotted at least one company that was acquired by a larger company. From my memory, one company in 2003 was acquired by IBM giving me more than 2 times return. In 2009, at least three companies were acquired giving me an average annualized return of over 200%.

Momentum strategy rewards us best from the end of the early recovery phase to the peak phase. The up phase started in 2004 for the 2000 market cycle and 2010 in the 2007 market cycle.

Note. The parameters of SMA-200, SMA-350, SMA-90, etc. and RSI are different for market exit/reentry, correction exit and individual stocks. These are the guidelines only. Stocks are more volatile than the market and are very different among them. Hence, define the 'days' according to the historical pattern of the individual stock and how often you trade them.

Filler: My translation from my Chinese friend's poem
When you understand "everything is changing", you won't be boosting your achievements. Today's splendid life could be a mess tomorrow.

When you understand "everything is changing", you won't be sad. Today's gloom could turn into sunshine tomorrow.

When you understand "everything is changing", you know today's gain could be tomorrow's loss and vice versa.

When you understand "everything is changing", there is no need to react to today's loss, gain, happiness and sadness.

#Filler: The Perils of Speculation
History shows that speculators often win big—only to lose everything.
Just look at the graveyard of hedge funds that soared high before crashing spectacularly.
A few rules to live by:
- **Avoid excessive leverage**—that includes leveraged ETFs and overextended margin accounts. What goes up fast can come down faster.

- **Time the market wisely**—if you must time it at all. Emotional trading usually backfires.
- **Stay invested**—bull markets last longer than bear markets. The patient investor who rides out the dips tends to win in the long run.

Speculation is a shortcut to wealth—but too often, the shortcut leads off a cliff.

Link: Making money during a crash.
https://www.youtube.com/watch?v=DjDCg4750dw

Sectors for market stages:
https://www.youtube.com/watch?v=FRdeXgf0rN8

3   Profitable Early Recovery

During a Market Plunge

A **market plunge** is the period between the **market peak and its bottom**, usually lasting **one to two years**. If you suspect a plunge is beginning, consider the following based on your risk tolerance:

1. **Cash is a Position**
   Contrary to popular belief, moving to cash is a valid strategy. You'll need it to re-enter equities later.
2. **Shift to Value Over Momentum**
   Reduce new purchases. Sell overvalued or momentum-driven stocks. For every two or three stocks I sell, I only buy one replacement during this phase.
3. **Use Stop Orders Cautiously**
   One of the few times I use stop orders is during a plunge. If you monitor the market daily, you can use market orders at predefined levels instead.
4. **Consider Contra ETFs**
   Aggressive investors can profit from falling markets using inverse ETFs.
5. **Covered Calls**
   Instead of holding declining stocks, I often prefer to sell. But if you want to hold, generating income with covered calls is a good compromise.
6. **Tax-Sensitive Investors**
   Older investors may not want to realize large capital gains

or give up dividend-paying stocks. Protective options strategies may be a better fit for them.

After the Plunge

Avoid buying aggressively in the first year after the peak—unless the deals are too good to ignore. Instead:

- Close short positions, sell put options, and unwind contra ETFs.
- Recognize that **investor psychology lags**: people often sell into early rallies out of fear.
- Focus on **interest rates**: if rates remain high, it's a great time to buy **high-yield (junk) bonds**, assuming the issuing companies are financially stable. Avoid mistakes like investing in GM bonds before its 2009 bankruptcy.

Personally, I prefer to wait until my **technical indicators** (like the SMA chart) confirm it's time to return to stocks. Fear often keeps investors on the sidelines, but the market always recovers—eventually.

Even during downturns, some **defensive sectors**—like healthcare, consumer staples, utilities, and pharmaceuticals—perform relatively well. Avoid **cyclical stocks**, including those in housing, autos, and consumer discretionary, as they're hit hardest in recessions.

Early Recovery and Beyond

The **early recovery phase** (like in 2003 and 2009) offers the best opportunities. Look for:

- **Beaten-down stocks** with strong fundamentals.
- **Bottom-fishing opportunities**, especially in companies that can survive another year or two.
- Acquisition targets: big firms often buy smaller, struggling companies to expand capabilities.

In 2003, one of my picks was acquired by IBM for a 2x gain. In 2009, three companies I bought were acquired, yielding an annualized return over 200%.

Traditional metrics like P/E may not apply here because many companies are still reporting losses. Instead, focus on **cash reserves**

vs. burn rate—if a company has enough cash to last two years, it might be a strong recovery candidate.

Momentum Strategy in Uptrend Phases

Momentum investing works best from the **end of early recovery to the market peak**. This phase started in 2004 after the 2000 crash and in 2010 after the 2008 crisis.

A Note on Technical Parameters

Technical indicators like **SMA-200, SMA-350, SMA-90**, and **RSI** vary by purpose:

- Use **longer SMAs** (like SMA-350) for market exits and entries.
- Use **shorter SMAs** for corrections or individual stocks.

Stocks are more volatile than the market, so tailor your charting parameters to each stock's historical behavior and your trading frequency.

Links:

Bottom fishing:

https://www.youtube.com/watch?v=hANAn9szRBA

Recommended stocks for Q3 2022. Understand why.

https://www.youtube.com/watch?v=4lxS7pfGukM

4   A non-correlation of the market and business

Market and Business Cycle: Understanding the Non-Correlation

The Business Cycle, also known as the Economic Cycle, typically lags behind the Market Cycle by approximately six months, as the stock market is considered a leading indicator of economic activity. However, as of May 2013, this pattern has not been evident. The U.S. economy has not aligned with the stock market's recovery, a divergence that is rarely observed. Despite the stock market recovering its losses from the 2007-2008 financial crisis and reaching new highs, the economy continues to struggle with high unemployment, under-employment, and weak GDP growth.

The interconnectivity of global economies further complicates the recovery, as many U.S. trade partners are also facing economic challenges. Although there have been modest signs of recovery within the U.S., employment rates may never return to their pre-recession levels. As of March 2016, the divergence between market performance and economic conditions persists.

Does This Divergence Matter to Retail Investors?

From an economic standpoint, the Economic Cycle is crucial as it predicts GDP growth, employment rates, and overall business health. However, for retail investors, the Market Cycle holds more importance as it directly impacts portfolio appreciation. Economists aim to forecast economic trends, while investors focus on capitalizing on market trends.

This non-correlation may persist for the foreseeable future, forcing economists to rethink their reliance on the Market Cycle as a predictor of economic performance. As long as the stock market continues its upward trajectory, most investors remain unbothered by the disconnect. However, historical patterns suggest that market and economic correlations will eventually realign.

Factors Contributing to the Non-Correlation

Several underlying factors contribute to the current disconnection between the market and the economy:

1. **Globalization of Large Corporations:**
   Many large corporations now operate on a global scale, with substantial revenue generated from international markets. This shift reduces the impact of U.S. economic conditions on the stock market, as multinational corporations (MNCs) prioritize profits from regions offering lower labor costs, tax incentives, and favorable government policies.

2. **Excessive Government Intervention:**
   The government has intervened extensively by bailing out companies that were on the brink of failure during the recession. This created a perception that certain companies were "too big to fail," leading to market speculation that future government intervention would protect stocks. Additionally, no significant actions were taken against executives and financial institutions responsible for the financial crisis, undermining market discipline.

3. **Easy Access to Capital:**
   In response to the financial crisis, banks were infused with government funds intended to stimulate the economy. However, instead of lending to small businesses and homeowners, banks directed their resources toward financing investors, fueling stock market growth. Moreover, reduced demand from businesses and homebuyers led to increased cash reserves within financial institutions.

4. **Corporate Stock Buybacks and High Cash Reserves:**
   Many corporations currently hold record-high cash reserves. Rather than investing in growth or expanding their workforce, companies are using these funds to buy back shares, acquire competitors, and increase dividend payouts. These practices artificially inflate stock prices, creating a misleading impression of market health.

5. **Government Debt and Market Perception:**
   The U.S. government has significantly increased its debt, which temporarily boosts market performance. However, long-term debt servicing limits economic growth and weakens the country's global competitiveness. Over time, the burden of debt repayment will fall on taxpayers, posing challenges for future economic stability.

6. **Regulatory Challenges:**
   Stringent government regulations, such as the Affordable Care Act (Obamacare), have discouraged small business growth and job creation. Increased regulatory costs make it difficult for businesses to expand or hire, further straining economic recovery.
7. **Market Perception as a Commodity:**
   The stock market is increasingly perceived as a commodity, driven by external factors such as currency depreciation, global conflicts, or resource discoveries like shale energy. Such influences push market trends in directions that do not align with domestic economic performance.

What Can Be Done?

To bridge the gap between market performance and economic growth, the following measures must be considered:

- **Reduce Excessive Government Spending:**
  Injecting large amounts of cash into the economy provides only short-term relief. Sustainable economic growth requires controlled spending and responsible fiscal policies.
- **Manage National Debt:**
  The U.S. government must prioritize debt management to maintain global competitiveness. Using a large portion of GDP to service debt hinders economic growth and reduces future financial flexibility.
- **Promote Job Creation:**
  Rather than expanding welfare programs, the government should focus on creating job opportunities. Providing incentives for businesses to hire workers will have a more significant and sustainable impact on economic growth.
- **Reduce Market Dependency on Government Intervention:**
  Allowing failing businesses to collapse naturally, rather than bailing them out, will restore market discipline and prevent artificially inflated stock prices.

Conclusion

Investing in a rising market may appear advantageous, especially during times of economic stagnation. However, the disconnect between market performance and economic health is unlikely to persist indefinitely. Ultimately, stock prices are driven by a company's ability to generate earnings. If corporate earnings fail to justify elevated stock prices, market corrections are inevitable.

Investors should continue to monitor P/E ratios, as they remain a reliable indicator of stock valuation. History suggests that market and economic correlations will eventually realign, reaffirming the fundamental relationship between the two cycles.

Afterthoughts

- There are many other correlations. The following should correlate with the economy: construction industry, employment, commodity /commodity-related currency and oil. Once a while and for a good reason, they do not.
- The market can only act as a leading indicator or proxy of economic activity if there is consensus on the direction. Sometimes what is coming in six months is fairly predictable but at other times when pundits are at odds the future course is fuzzy. So, market indices are really tracking where consensus "thinks" GDP is going'.

   To be clear a market index is a summary of where consensus believes the economy is headed and this sentiment is a proxy for forward earnings. For the playing stocks and not the index, it is their cumulative sentiment which acts as a guide.
- QE, printing money, foreign loans (to China...), reserve currency, debt ceiling all mean the same: Live in a higher standard of living than we can afford.
   When Uncle Sam unsuccessfully uses all the tools to maintain our living standard and being the world's policeman, he runs out of tools. That will build a higher cliff for us to fall.
   Hopefully, shale energy will save our economy.
- The global economy still has not recovered as of July, 2013 according to this article.
   (http://www.telegraph.co.uk/finance/economics/10174862/Rene wed-fear-of-global-recession-as-companies-rein-in-spending-plans.html)
- Here are some economic indicators.
   http://en.wikipedia.org/wiki/Economic_indicator

- This time is REALLY different. Your Dad's generation does not have the internet, powerful PC, low-interest commission, trading at a click of the mouse… Global economies are better connected via the internet, shipping… All these affect our lives and economies.

5   A tale of two market plunges

I gather the data of the last two plunges (2000 and 2007) and check out what they have in common.

All the data are for information and education purposes only and so are the conclusions. All market plunges are different but some common characteristics do exist. Market plunges older than 2000 may not be useful as the market conditions then were very different from today's market.

Charts
The first one is for 2007 and the next one for 2000.
The following charts are also saved in the following link in case you read this book on a small screen. Type the following link in your browser to display the graph on your PC if desirable.
http://ebmyth.blogspot.com/2013/07/chart-market-plunge-2007.html

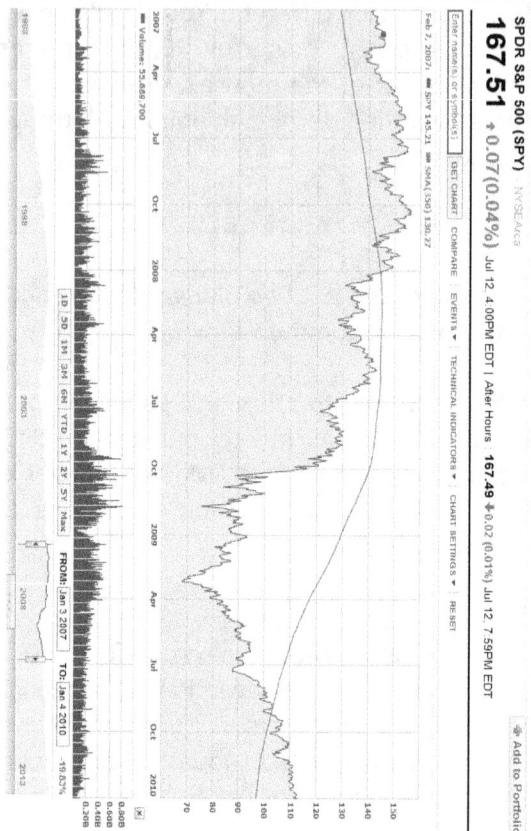

2007 Market Plunge Chart from Yahoo!Finance

Explanations:
- The red line is the 350-day SMA (simple moving average for the last 350 trade sessions). Sell when the price is below the SMA and buy when it is above the SMA. It gives us the exit point from the market and the reentry point to the market
- This chart uses SPY, an ETF simulating the S&P 500 index. A total market ETF would be a better choice unless you only trade the S&P 500 stocks. If most of your stocks are in small caps, use an index ETF for small caps. Instead of using an ETF, you can use any market index.
- The exit point is Jan. 7, 2008 (a brief indicator in Nov., 2007). Either exit point is fine. We should start to exit the market on Nov. 26, 2007 and this market plunge was nice to give us one more exit point. In reality, it takes us more time to exit the market totally. It looks like a double peak to me in technical terms.
- It is not possible to catch the peak from the chart (July – October, 2007), but this chart helps us to prevent further and bigger losses. I have researched to find the common metrics for peaks and bottoms. They have not been proven so far in my tests.

- The return to the market is around September, 2009 from the chart (above the 350 SMA). I returned to stocks in February, 2009, right at the bottom. It is just pure luck, my timing was based on the duration after the plunge, or many other factors that I may have forgotten. That's one reason we should take notes and learn from our experiences.
- Enlarge the chart by selecting a shorter date range or using a larger screen.

The following graph displays the same for the 2000 market plunge. If you have a problem in viewing it on the small screen, display it on your PC screen via the same link above. It is better to produce it yourself using Yahoo!Finance or one of the many sites to produce SMA charts.

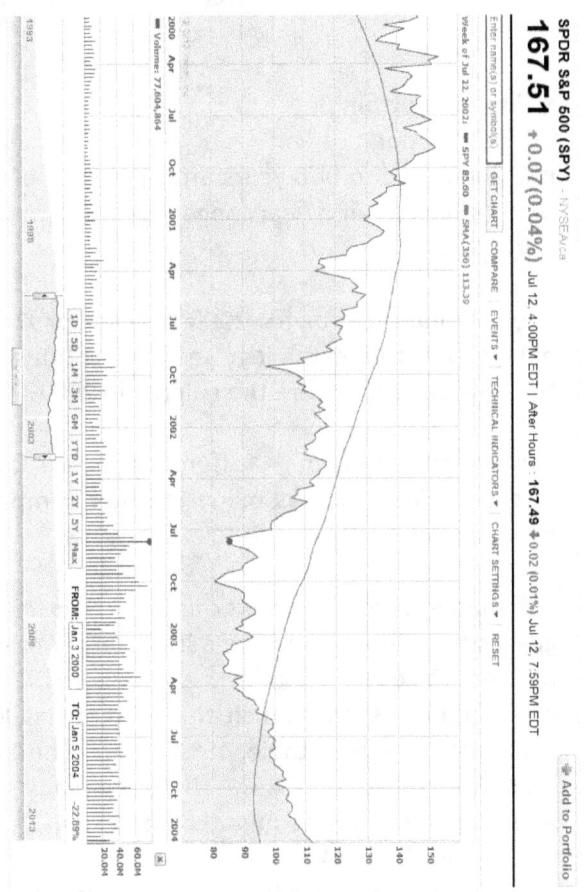

2000 Market Plunge Chart from Yahoo!Finance

Significant Periods

All the durations are estimates. They are different in each market plunge.

- Plunging period.

  It is the period between the start of the plunge (i.e., the peak) and the bottom. On the average, the duration of the plunge is about a year. Do not buy stocks during this period except selling shorts and buying contra ETFs to the market for aggressive investors.

- Early Recovery.

  It is the period between the market bottom and the mid part of the recovery and usually it starts one and a half year after the plunge.

Detecting the bottom

1. By the duration.

   It is about one to two years after the start of the plunge. It takes at least half a year longer for the offending sector(s) to recover.

   The offending sector for 2000 (the sector that caused the plunge) was the technology sector. The housing sector and the finance sector were the culprits in 2007.

   Some of the stocks in the offending sectors lose most or all of their values such as many internet companies in 2000 and Lehman Brothers in 2007.

   The market recovered faster in 2007 than 2000 due to the government intervention by excessively printing money

2. By the total loss.

   Another hint is how much the market has lost from the peak. From the next table, 45% is a good bet. I start buying on 40% loss instead of 45%. There are many great bargains and we do not want to miss the opportunities.

3. By the 350-day SMA.

   For more conservative investors, wait for the stock price to pass the 350-day SMA (or other SMA such as the 200-day SMA). The 'day' is the last trade session.

All the market stages can seldom be predicted precisely. We are responsible for our own actions. Your actions also depend on your risk tolerance. A conservative investor would leave the market entirely on the first hint and return to the market slowly and gradually after the first hint.

Offending Sectors
Usually the offending sectors (the sectors that cause the bubble to burst) take at least 2 years to recover. Try out the SMA-350 and SMA-200 charts on the ETFs of these offending sectors.

ETFs and more articles on the offending sectors:

2007: Housing ETF XHB and Financial ETF XLF.
       Housing bubble.
(http://en.wikipedia.org/wiki/United_States_housing_bubble)

2000: Technology ETF XLK and Telecommunication IYZ.
       Internet bubble.
(http://en.wikipedia.org/wiki/Dot-com_bubble)

Depending on which report you read, the dates will not be exact. Some claim the housing crisis started in 2008 instead of 2007 and the internet crisis started in 2001 instead of 2000.

Summary by tables
Again, the dates are not exact and they depend on an individual interpretation. My table indicates 51% average loss and I use 45% as a more conservative number. I use my own dates and interpretations on the following tables.

Table: Market Plunges

Market Plunge	Months (Peak to Bottom)	Loss	Annualized loss
2000	17	56%	40%
2007	25	47%	23%
Average	21	51%	31%

Table: Vital Dates

Market Plunge	Peak	Bottom	Indicator Exit	Indicator Reenter
2000	08/28/00	09/20/02	10/30/00	05/26/03
2007	10/12/07	03/06/09	01/03/08	09/08/09

Most investors were fully invested in 2007 and 2008 and NOT fully invested in 2009. If you followed the exit indicator and reenter indicator, you should do far better than the average investor.

Afterthoughts

- Many including myself do not believe a market plunge is coming as of 7/2014. However, we have to be careful with the following analysis. Run the simple chart to spot any indication of a market plunge at least once a month. The following are from my experiences.

    o Among my top-performing screens for the last 3 months, many top-performing screens are from the peak stage (defined by me) rather than other stages in a market cycle.
    o The typical market cycle is about 5 years. It has been about 6 years since 2007.
    o The stock market has not reached the bubble stage yet. It will if it continues to rise at this pace in 2014.

- On 6/20/2013, the market lost more than 2% in a day due to the Fed indicating no more easy money. The bond yield jumped. The Fed has been dumping about 1 trillion a year. When the money stops, the market would crash and the 2% loss seems to be a canary. Hopefully the current correction would be less than 10%

    [Update: only 6%]. Wall Street depends on the government handouts and the government is running out of tools to fix the economy.

- Some REITs are inversely affected by the rising interest rate. http://seekingalpha.com/article/1570772-american-capital-mortgage-investment-was-the-baby-thrown-out-with-the-bathwater
- Will the market go even higher as of 6/2014? We have to compare the risk / reward ratio. If the risk is too high, we may want to take some chips off the table.
- To me, there are 4 groups of investors.
    1. Institutional investors. Their performances vary. In short, hedge funds as a group have not beaten the market in the last 5 years.

2. Mutual funds. Most cannot do market timing from their own regulations and as a group they do not beat the market after expenses.
3. Retail investors are always on the wrong side of the market via fear and greed.
4. While investors from #1 to #3 are losers, there must be some winners beating the market as a trade is a zero-sum game.

   In theory, we cannot beat the mutual fund managers who have better resources. However, we can use market timing to our advantage.

6   Secular bull market is coming?

Understanding Secular Stock Markets and Market Cycles

My definition: A secular stock market is a prolonged period, typically lasting between 12 to 22 years, during which the market trends consistently in one direction. These periods can either be secular bull markets, where prices generally rise, or secular bear markets, where prices consistently decline.

Within a secular market, shorter market cycles also occur, typically lasting around five years. However, there are exceptions; for example, the market cycle from 2000 to 2007 lasted about seven years, and the current one from 2007 to 2016 has lasted eight years so far.

Additionally, within a single year, there are usually two mini market cycles, characterized by 5% corrections or surges. Sometimes there is one correction of around 5% and another between 5% to 15%. These short-term fluctuations present strategic opportunities to buy stocks during dips and sell during surges, assuming there are no major market plunges.

The durations of secular markets, market cycles, and yearly corrections are not scientifically precise but rather rough estimates based on historical trends. For simplicity, a 20-year period is often used to define a secular market, though 15 years may be a more accurate average.

Differentiating Market Cycles from Economic Cycles

Investors should understand the difference between market cycles and economic cycles (also known as business cycles). Market cycles are crucial for investors, while economic cycles are more relevant to economists and business leaders. Historically, the secular economic cycle tends to lag behind the secular market cycle by an average of six months, except for the current period (2007-2016).

Predicting the Next Secular Bull Market
It is often the case that predictions made by well-known individuals about the economy or stock market receive widespread media attention. However, lesser-known individuals making predictions may go unnoticed. Despite this, I predict that the next secular bull market could commence as early as 2018. If it does not, it would be important to identify errors in my reasoning or unexpected events that may have influenced the outcome.
Timing market shifts is always a challenge. Acting too early in a secular bull market can lead to premature losses, while reacting too late can result in missed profit opportunities. The same logic applies to secular bear markets.

Historical Secular Markets
The relationship between market performance and economic conditions is clear. In a healthy market, the economy thrives, creating employment opportunities and fostering widespread prosperity. However, globalization has changed the employment landscape as companies can now hire labor at the lowest cost from around the world.

Here are the approximate periods for the past three secular markets:
- Secular Bear Market: 1960-1980
- Secular Bull Market: 1980-2000
- Secular Bear Market: 2000-2020

Secular markets before 1960 were not included due to significantly different economic conditions.

During a secular bull market, almost all investors see their portfolios grow, and consumer spending increases. In times of war, the market tends to decline, except for industries directly involved in defense production.
The Role of War in Secular Markets

One of the primary drivers of secular bear markets is war, while the absence of war often contributes to secular bull markets. Historical evidence supports this observation:

- In the 1960s, the Vietnam War and its aftermath contributed to the secular bear market.
- More recently, the wars in the Middle East have consumed vast resources, impacting economic growth.

When wars end, resources shift back to the economy, fostering growth. Additionally, political reluctance to engage in new conflicts can sustain economic prosperity, as seen in the bull market from 1980 to 2000.

Market plunges are often triggered by economic bubbles, which eventually correct themselves. For instance, the dot-com bubble in 2000 and the housing bubble in 2007 resulted from excessive valuations and easy credit availability. Following these market plunges, recessions typically ensue.

Government intervention plays a crucial role in mitigating market downturns. Proactive measures to identify and manage economic bubbles can prevent severe market crashes.

Future Outlook for Secular Bull Markets

While I anticipate the next secular bull market starting in 2018, several potential challenges could delay its onset until 2020 or later:

- Potential military conflicts with China over Taiwan or other regional disputes.
- Disruptions caused by global climate change, impacting food supply and water availability.
- Natural disasters such as major earthquakes or hurricanes.
- Persistent budget deficits and excessive government spending, potentially leading to economic instability.

However, certain positive developments, such as increased domestic energy production through trapped gas and oil extraction, could accelerate economic recovery and facilitate the start of a secular bull market.

Conclusion

Investors should remain pragmatic and adjust their strategies based on ongoing developments. While predictions about market trends are inherently uncertain, a careful analysis of economic and geopolitical events can improve investment decisions.

Regardless of market conditions, opportunities always exist within market cycles. During secular bull markets, adopting a more aggressive investment strategy is beneficial, while a conservative approach is advisable during secular bear markets.

Ultimately, understanding the interplay between economic policies, global conflicts, and market trends is essential for navigating the ever-changing financial landscape.

Afterthoughts
- Signs of an economy recovery:
    1. Increase corporate profits.
    2. Increase employment.
    3. Increase housing starts.
    4. Decrease Federal deficit.
    5. Increase the growth of GDP.
    6. Rising values in some sectors such as consumers, high tech., housing, etc.

    As of 1/2014, #2 and #3 seem to be improving. #1 is OK. However, #4 is not.

    When you borrow money (#4) and use it productively, you can improve #1 to #3. I have strong doubts about this economic recovery.

    We're having a non-correlation in the Economy and the market.

- Traditional theory would say a 20-years secular cycle with 10 years between the major pullbacks. The first major pullback was called the Capital Crisis (1997-2003). The second major pullback was called the Real Estate Crisis (2007-2009). According to this theory, the next major pullback will be 2017 (Capital Crisis).

- In between major crises are business cycle pullbacks (Kitchen Cycle) approximately 5 years each. These are also called inventory cycles.

  It should be noted that these have always existed, even before Capitalism in 1720. During the secular bull market, they are muted by the positive market trend. However, they still exist.

- Norman believes we have started the secular bull market on Jan. 1, 2013. The secular 20-year cycle is based on the generations. The X generation has just moved into old age and the millennials are becoming mid-life consumers--This is a huge generation, similar to the Baby Boomers and demand for everything is going up.

- Nikolai Kondratiev would say the generational economic cycle has 4 seasons. He said it lasted 50-60 years. http://en.wikipedia.org/wiki/Nikolai_Kondratiev

#Filler: Rethinking Success in Life
Contrary to popular belief, success isn't measured by how many friends you have—or how many stocks you hold. It's about how you *use* your toys:
- You're **wise** if you pass away surrounded by gadgets you actually enjoyed.
- You're **a bit foolish** if you never upgrade them.
- You're **wasting potential** if your money just sits idle instead of turning into something fun or useful.
- And you're **truly brilliant** when you share your toys—like Gates and Buffett, who've figured out that giving can be the most rewarding play of all.

7   Market prediction for a new year

This article demonstrates how I predict the market to be. It is for 2013, but the logic is valid for predictions about the future market.

In the article "My prediction for 2013 – all other predictions will be wrong", Larry Smith, a respected contributor at Seeking Alpha, suggested that many yearly predictions on 2012 by known organizations and famed individuals are often wrong.

Larry said,

"To prove my point, I thought I would look at some of the 2012 market forecasts that were made at the end of 2011. Let's start by looking at some of the S&P 500 forecasts that were made by the leading Wall Street firms. **Morgan Stanley** (MS) takes the worst prediction prize by forecasting an end-of-year the S&P 500 closing price of 1167, off by almost 300 points. **Goldman Sachs** (GS) predicted 1250 as the closing price of the S&P 500 price and **Seabreeze Partners** misfired on the high end by forecasting the S&P 500 closing price of 1527. Click here to see all the major brokerage firms' predictions for 2012. Most of the firms underestimated the size of the stock market rise."

I agree with him completely, but there are exceptions and I try to be one of them. We can profit a lot from an accurate prediction. We need a prediction to be a framework on how we want to invest for the year and adjust the prediction as events surface.

My past prediction

Why should you want to follow a prediction from a nobody like me? My predictions have been on track many times, particularly for the year 2000, 2003 and 2009. In 2012, SPY (similar to the S&P 500 index) had a return of 13%. My prediction is 10%, off by 3%.

2013 is harder to predict and it depends on whether we have a QEn and the interest rates that have no way to go but up. We've been up too much since 2009 and the economy is still off with poor employment rates

8   What to do at mid-year

Market patterns often shift midway through the year. While the following approach isn't foolproof—and may fall into the "data-fitting" trap—it has shown promise in past years. I include it here with the intention to refine or validate it through continued testing.

Mid-Year Adjustment Logic

From observation, when the market **overreacts in the first half**—either positively or negatively—it often **rebalances in the second half**. But this doesn't always happen. There are two schools of thought on how to respond mid-year:

1. **Contrarian Approach**
   If the market has surged well above its expected annual return by mid-year, reduce your equity exposure or take profits. I belong to this camp.
2. **Momentum Approach**
   Let your winners run and stay aligned with the existing trend.

These are essentially **opposite strategies**, and each has merit depending on your investment style and the current market context.

2012: A Case Study

In 2012, I projected a 10% gain for the S&P 500 (SPY). By mid-year, SPY was already up 7%. Using a simple formula:

Remaining gain = Projected return – YTD return
$\rightarrow 10\% - 7\% = 3\%$

Based on this, I stayed invested, anticipating a modest 3% gain through year-end. The actual return from July to December was about 6%, making this strategy successful in that instance.

General Guidance (with Caution)

If the market has already captured most or all of its projected annual gain by June or July:

- **Be cautious**; the upside may be limited.
- **If underperforming** relative to expectations, it may be an opportunity to add exposure.

Regardless, **mid-year is a great time to rebalance**:

- Review sector weightings.
- Assess risk of a market correction.
- Look for opportunities created by volatility or missed dips.

This isn't a hard rule, but a loose guideline worth observing and adjusting over time. It's about **increasing your probability of success**, not guaranteeing it.

9   The worst-case scenario in market timing

One of the biggest risks in market timing is what I call the **whipsaw effect**: you exit the market based on valid warning signals, only to watch it continue climbing. You grow frustrated, re-enter near the top—and then the market crashes.

How to Avoid the Worst Timing Mistake
To manage this risk, take a **tiered and cautious approach**:

- **Step 1: Scale Out Gradually**
  On your first signal of a potential market plunge, **move a portion** of your holdings—especially higher-risk stocks—to cash. The percentage depends on your risk tolerance.
- **Step 2: Incremental Exits**
  If you still expect the market to rise a bit more (say 2%), set sell targets **slightly above current prices**. Gradually raise cash while the market climbs.
- **Step 3: Full Exit Upon Strong Signals**
  When multiple signals align or the plunge begins, consider a more aggressive exit. Personally, my "sell all" scenario typically applies to **about 50% of my portfolio**—not because I distrust my strategy, but because I don't go "all in" on any one outcome. That's just how I manage risk.

Conservative Investors: A Different Playbook
For those relying on investments for income or close to retirement:

- Consider staying in **cash during the peak stage** of the cycle.
- Rotate into **long-term bonds** when interest rates are high.
- Re-enter the stock market **only near the bottom** of the cycle.
  This is a boring strategy—but often a highly effective one with **less stress and lower risk**. While it may underperform in bull markets, it can outperform over a full cycle due to avoided losses.

Don't Forget: False Signals Happen
Even if the market does not plunge after you exit, the strategy can still work if you follow reentry indicators. These false signals may cause you to miss a few percentage points—but that's the **cost of insurance** against far larger losses.

Section III: Correction

1   Correction

Understanding Market Timing

Market timing is often misunderstood. However, identifying major market plunges can be straightforward with a simple analytical approach.

On the other hand, detecting market corrections is more complex. My track record has shown more successful predictions than failures in recognizing these corrections.

Defining a Market Correction

Different investors have varying definitions of market corrections. My criteria for defining a correction are as follows:

- A decline of 10% or more from the peak within the last 180 days.
- A drop of more than 5% within a month.
- Some corrections extend to a 20% loss.

A market plunge, in contrast, involves a loss of 40% or more from the recent peak to the lowest point. The area between a 20% and 40% loss remains ambiguous.

Market Corrections: Trends and Opportunities

Based on my definition, there was no correction in 2013, which is a rare occurrence. On average, at least one correction happens each year since 2000. Additionally, minor corrections of around 5% occur twice a year in the absence of a 10% correction.

Corrections offer prime buying opportunities, while temporary peaks present selling opportunities. Historically, peaks and corrections appear one to two times per year, though their frequency varies. My strategy involves selling at expected peaks and buying at anticipated lows, adjusting cash reserves according to risk tolerance. Long-term investors following a "buy-and-hold" strategy can disregard corrections altogether.

Indicators of Market Peaks

While not always reliable, the following indicators can signal a potential market peak:

- The market gains over 10% of the expected annual return early in the year. For instance, if the projected return is 12% for the year and the market reaches this by March, it may indicate a peak.
- The market surpasses the previous peak by a significant margin, based on individual risk tolerance.
- The annualized market P/E ratio (e.g., SPY ETF) exceeds its 5-year or 10-year average.
- Foreign markets decline while domestic markets rise significantly.
- Interest rates increase, typically leading to market declines.
- A three-day streak where advancing stocks outnumber declining stocks.
- A three-day streak where new highs surpass new lows.
- The SPY ETF's 200-day Simple Moving Average (SMA) exceeds its price by more than 10%, suggesting a temporary peak.
- The Relative Strength Index (RSI-14) of SPY exceeds 55%, indicating an overbought condition.

These signals should be used as reference points, as no single metric guarantees market direction.

Causes of Market Corrections

Market corrections occur for various reasons, including:

- Overvalued market conditions
- Rising interest rates
- Declining corporate earnings
- Economic uncertainties such as trade wars

Conclusion

Compared to market plunges, corrections are more challenging to identify. Since 2000, my methodology has successfully recognized major downturns.

Investors should exercise caution and avoid placing their entire portfolio at risk during a correction. It is advisable to keep no more than 25% of the portfolio in cash at expected peaks.

When the market corrects, it presents a buying opportunity. However, in the event of a market plunge, exiting the market becomes necessary to mitigate losses. If multiple indicators exceed the following thresholds, the market is likely reaching its peak:

Indicator	Threshold
SMA-50	4%
SMA-200%	6%

SMA-350%	11%
Average of SMAs	9%
RSI (14)	65%

By carefully monitoring these indicators, investors can make informed decisions to navigate market fluctuations effectively.

2   Signs of a correction

Identifying a Market Correction

Several indicators suggest that the market may be peaking and overbought. SPY, an ETF that mirrors the S&P 500, shows an RSI(14) of 67% and an SMA-200% of 8.35% as of June 29, 2014. The SMA-200% reflects how much the stock price deviates from its 200-day simple moving average.

While some investors dismiss technical analysis, institutional fund managers often rely on it to guide their decisions. Hedge fund managers, in particular, use it as a tool to manage risk. Although mutual fund managers are restricted from market timing due to regulatory constraints, hedge funds have more flexibility in this regard.

Market Trends and the Likelihood of a Correction

Newton's Law humorously reminds us that what goes up must come down. The market has consistently risen over time, even accounting for inflation, but periodic pullbacks are inevitable. Small declines are termed corrections, while more severe drops are considered market plunges.

Historically, the market experiences at least one 10% correction per year, alongside approximately 1.5 corrections of 5% or more. Since no 10% correction occurred in 2013, the likelihood of one happening soon increases. Many experts incorrectly predicted a correction in 2013, but it is rare for such forecasts to be wrong two years in a row.

Currently, there are more articles predicting a correction than disputing one. This widespread belief may become a self-fulfilling prophecy, driven by herd mentality.

Another indicator is low market volume and narrow trading ranges over several days, often signaling an impending shift. Just as the sea is calmest before a storm, market quietness can precede turbulence.

From a valuation standpoint, the market appears fully priced. Even if no correction occurs, potential profits seem limited relative to risk. For risk-averse investors, protecting gains and securing peace of mind may be preferable to chasing the final increment of profit.

Strategies for Protection

How you prepare depends on your risk tolerance:

- **Increase Cash Holdings:** Hold between 0% and 50% in cash, with 15% being a balanced recommendation. Those ignoring correction signals may opt for 0%, while conservative investors might favor 50%.

- **Use Stop Orders:** Set stop-loss orders and adjust them as stock prices rise. Since corrections can be brief, stop orders are more effective during significant market downturns than in minor corrections.

- **Short the Market Cautiously:** While shorting is generally not advisable, a contra ETF could offer a hedge. However, only risk money you can afford to lose.

- **Utilize Options:** Options can serve as portfolio protection in uncertain market conditions.

- **Prepare a Watchlist:** Identify stocks to buy in the event of a correction and wait for a better entry point.

It is essential to remember that predictions, including mine, are not certainties. Just as we purchase insurance without expecting to use it, market predictions serve as precautions rather than guarantees.

Final Thoughts

Market timing is an inexact science, but the goal is to be more right than wrong.

Reader responses tend to fall into two camps: those who believe in market timing and those who do not. Regardless of what happens in the next few months, I neither take credit for being correct nor accept blame if no correction occurs. My track record suggests more accurate than inaccurate predictions, but past success does not ensure future accuracy.

Additional factors, such as interest rates, oil prices, and geopolitical events, have also been discussed. Interest rates are expected to rise by year-end, while recent oil price increases stem from Middle Eastern conflicts. Current geopolitical tensions, including in Ukraine and the Middle East, seem unlikely to influence markets significantly, given the U.S. administration's reluctance to intervene.

While I do not foresee a market plunge exceeding 30%—as bubble stocks remain relatively scarce—I predict that these stocks will fall to half their 2013 and 2014 peaks by year-end. Ultimately, every stock trade is a prediction, some of which materialize while others do not.

Detecting corrections is more challenging than identifying plunges. If a major downturn occurs, my focus will shift primarily to protecting my portfolio.

3   Anticipating a correction

Anticipating a Market Correction
If you follow a **buy-and-hold** investment strategy, you can skip this section. However, for active investors, this chapter builds on the previous one by providing insights into preparing for a potential market correction.

Strategic Selling and Buying
To maximize portfolio gains, consider selling a portion of your stocks before a market correction and repurchasing them during or after the downturn. While this strategy is not foolproof, it can

enhance portfolio appreciation—though at the cost of capital gains taxes in non-retirement accounts.

Indicators of an Impending Market Correction
Certain patterns suggest a market downturn may be approaching:
- The market has been on a steady rise for more than **four months** since the last dip.
- The market has exceeded its expected growth threshold.
- Many of your stocks have reached their peak—this could be an opportunity to lock in profits.
- **Technical Analysis**: Use stock charts to assess trends and identify potential reversals.

Using Simple Moving Averages (SMA) for Predictions
One useful tool for predicting market movements is the **Simple Moving Average (SMA)**. The general strategy:
- **Buy** when the stock price is above the **SMA**.
- **Sell** when the stock price falls below the **SMA**.

For instance, an **SMA-50** (50-day moving average) was a useful indicator in 2012. However, varying the number of days (e.g., using **SMA-100**) or incorporating additional indicators can help reduce market noise and improve trading frequency based on your investment style.

For a real-world example, visit:
http://ebmyth.blogspot.com/2013/09/correction-example.html

In some cases, short-term fluctuations can lead to excessive trading, as seen in April of the referenced example. A longer trend, such as the one from **July 1 to October 15**, offers a clearer view of sustained market movement.

By carefully adjusting your strategy and leveraging the right technical tools, you can better navigate market corrections and position your portfolio for long-term growth.

Example using a chart

Here is one of the charts that could predict temporary market dips and surges. Buy when the price is above the SMA (simple moving average) and sell when it is below. This example uses 50 days for SMA for 2012. SMA-50 is also available from Finviz.com.

Vary the number of days and/or use other indicators to reduce noise or improve the trading frequency to fit your individual needs.

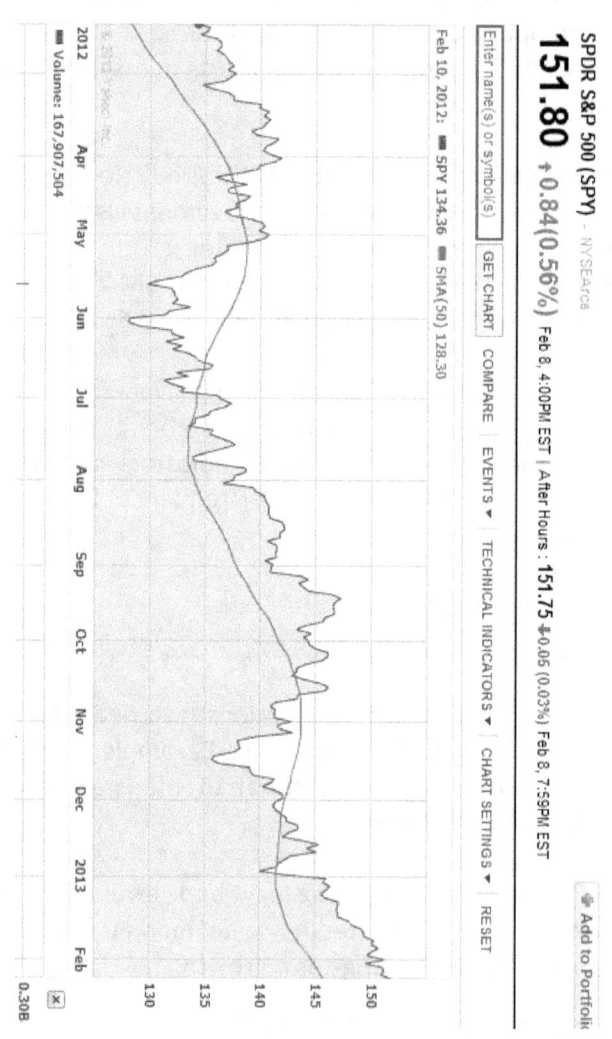

Source: Yahoo!Finance.

If you are reading this book on a small screen and cannot see the chart, type the following into your browser.
http://ebmyth.blogspot.com/2013/09/correction-example.html

There are too many trades in the above chart especially in the month of April. The period from July 1 to Oct. 15 is a good capture of the upward trend. It is useful but not perfect. Try to use SMA-100 instead of the above SMA-50.

Example of a market top

The following is from my blog written on May 19, 2011 and it turned out to be quite accurate. Check why I expected a correction would be coming. Hopefully we can spot the next one with similar reasoning. However, there is no guarantee for future performance and predictions.

Click here on the actual blog and the summary follows.
http://www.tonyp4idea.blogspot.com/2011/05/anticipating-correction.html

As of May 19, 2011, the market had been up by about 9% YTD. The experts were divided on whether the market would take a correction with convincing arguments for and against.

I had been selling stocks several weeks before and moved most of my Annuity positions to a money market fund. My total cash was 25% and I was still selling. I tried to sell most of my stocks at 5 to 10% higher than the market prices. Hence, even if there were no correction, I was still selling far better than my current prices and it was a reasonable insurance policy. I predicted that the market was risky at that time; you have to trust your prediction and act accordingly as it did.

After I had accumulated more than 30% in cash, I played the 'Buy one and Sell two' strategy betting I could spot stocks better than others. I tried to sell the stocks I bought right away for a small profit as I still expected a correction.

* Arguments for no correction:

- QE3 would materialize (even it will not amount to a lot of cash due to the debt ceiling).
- Corporate profits are still rising.
- The economy is improving.

* Arguments for correction:

- QE3 will not be materialized and no money will be used to stimulate the economy.
- The market is taking a breather after 9% YTD (I expect 5% rise in mid-year).
- Slim chance for the rule 'Stay away in May' as it had not been working for the two consecutive years except in today's extended bull market.
- There are financial problems from China, EU, Japan and N. Africa.
- With tightening margin requirements on commodities, oil..., speculative trades will be reduced (good for the long term).

The above is a summary of what the experts said. I did not do any research (as it is already available from the web). I summarized their opinions, selected what made sense to me, and acted accordingly.

I chose the middle road by not taking extreme actions such as selling all my holdings and heavily investing in contra ETFs.

Afterthoughts

- My Elastic Band Theory.
  The more you stretch an elastic band, the more it will rebound. When a stock's timing score is 10 (the best), it has no way to go but down. That is similar to the general market.

  The risk/reward ratio is too high as of 4/2013. Unless you have a time machine, you may not want to make the last buck.
- A related article from SA.

(http://seekingalpha.com/article/1344071-5-reasons-why-i-am-shorting-the-market)

Links
Original blog:
http://www.tonyp4idea.blogspot.com/2011/05/anticipating-correction.html
An article on preparing for a correction.
http://www.forbes.com/sites/investor/2014/05/19/five-things-to-do-in-a-stock-market-correction/

#Filler: Roadblocks to progress

We use privacy to stop facial recognition. The device from Ring has reduced a lot of thefts and possibly crimes. Similar to stem cell research. That's why China is passing us in these areas.

4   Market correction example

I have 50% in cash before the August (2015) correction. I should have 100% if I followed my chart. However, we are just human beings blinded by our greed / fears and emotional attachment.

Stocks	Buy Price	Buy Date	Return	Sold date
Apple (AAPL)	107.20	08/26/15	12%	10/19/15
Gilead Sciences (GILD)	105.94	08/26/15	-4%	
General Motors (GM)	27.69	08/26/15	12%	09/17/15
Genwealth Financial (GNW)	4.54	08/26/15	10%	08/27/15

#Filler: Investment Returns

My good friends sold all their rental properties and shifted their focus to health and leisure in retirement. In contrast, I found myself losing sleep during the market plunge in early 2025—though, thankfully, it rebounded.

Another friend has children with high-paying jobs, the result of years of investment in their education. Even if my portfolio might be outperforming theirs on paper, I sometimes can't shake the feeling that I've come up short in more important ways.

Filler: Deflation
Deflation is worse than inflation for companies. When the company finds they have to sell the products at lower prices than expected, they have to cut down some products and lay off employees.

The main job of the Federal Reserve Bank is adjusting inflation/deflation to some acceptable levels.

Section IV: Market timing by Calendar

1   Market timing by calendar

Market Timing by Calendar: Historical Insights and Predictions
The following predictions are based on historical market data. Your findings may vary slightly depending on the time period you analyze. You can verify these trends by loading historical data for SPY (S&P 500 ETF) from Yahoo! Finance and comparing them to my predictions. These are my interpretations based on historical patterns and should be used as a reference only.

1. Presidential Election Cycle
Historically, the stock market tends to perform worse in the first two years after a presidential election compared to the latter two years. The **third year** of a presidential term is often the strongest for the market, as the incumbent administration typically works to stimulate the economy to gain voter support. This is often achieved through measures such as printing more money, lowering interest rates, and reducing taxes. Statistically, the third year is followed by a strong election year.

- **Pre-Election Period**: The 100 days leading up to the election are usually positive and less volatile, based on 40 years of data.
- **Post-Election Period**: The 100 days following the inauguration, often referred to as the "honeymoon period," also tend to be favorable for the market.

Interestingly, Democratic presidents have historically seen better market performance than Republican presidents, despite the latter being traditionally viewed as more pro-business.

2. Olympics Effect
Hosting the Olympics has been associated with positive stock market performance in the host country the year after the event. This could be due to increased global exposure and the economic boost from infrastructure investments.
- **Recent Examples**:
  - **United Kingdom (2012)**: The EWU ETF (UK-focused) gained 11% from January 3, 2013, to December 23, 2013.

- o **China (2008)**: The FXI ETF (China-focused) surged 43% from January 3, 2009, to December 31, 2009.

However, there are exceptions. For instance, Greece struggled after hosting the Olympics due to excessive spending on infrastructure that provided little long-term economic benefit. Similarly, Japan's 2020 Olympics were negatively impacted by the COVID-19 pandemic. Additionally, winning Olympic medals does not correlate with stock market performance, as evidenced by the dissolution of the Russian Empire and East Germany despite their Olympic successes.

3. Seasonal Trends

Historically, the best time to invest in the stock market is from **November 1 to April 30**. This aligns with the adage "Sell in May and go away," though this strategy has not been reliable since 2009 due to the market's recovery phase.

- **Summer Doldrums**: The summer months often see weaker market performance, possibly because investors sell stocks to fund vacations or college tuition. However, buying quality stocks during these dips can be profitable.
- **Worst Month**: September is historically the worst month for the market, followed by October. However, if October avoids a major crash, it can be an excellent time to buy stocks.
- **Best Months**: November is typically the strongest month for bull markets, with December also performing well. Many experts believe the best three-month period for the market begins in November.
- **Best 30 Days**: The period from **December 15 to January 15** has historically been strong, as seen in 2012-2013.

4. Window Dressing by Institutional Investors

Institutional investors often engage in "window dressing" around November 1, selling underperforming stocks and buying winners to improve their portfolio's appearance. On average, winners tend to outperform the market by 2%, while losers underperform by 1%.

- **Strategy for Winners**: Evaluate the top 10 performing stocks from the past 10 months or year-to-date (YTD) as of October 15. Consider selling them after a 3% gain or holding for two months.
- **Strategy for Losers**: In December, identify stocks that have lost more than 30% over the past 11 months or YTD. Sort them by earnings yield in descending order and evaluate the top 10. Buy these stocks and consider selling them three months later.

Important Notes:
- Avoid foreign stocks, stocks with low trading volumes, and those priced below $2.
- Do not invest during market downturns or in years with significant losses, such as 2007 and 2008.
- Always consider current events, such as potential wars or interest rate hikes, before making investment decisions.

Final Thoughts

These predictions are based on historical trends and should not be taken as guarantees. Market conditions can change, and external factors such as geopolitical events or economic policies can significantly impact performance. Use these insights as a guideline, but always prioritize current market conditions and your own research when making investment decisions

Afterthoughts

- I predict it will be a sideways market in the later part of 2013. I am following the sideways strategy: Buy on dips and sell when the market is up. One's prediction.

- Why September has a bad reputation?
  http://www.marketwatch.com/story/betting-on-septembers-terrible-odds-2013-08-27?dist=beforebell

  September of 2013 (2 days away at the time of this writing) may have more problems. Check out how many of the following are correct on Oc. 1, 2013. Use it as a future guideline to predict the next September using the current market conditions then:

1. The market is not excessively expensive, but it is not cheap. It is due for a 5% correction.
2. Unrest in Syria (check any unrest in your next prediction in September).
3. High oil prices due to Syria.
4. September is statistically a bad month for the stock market. However, it could be an opportunity to invest after the correction if any.
5. Interest rates are rising.
6. All the above indicate the market will dip. However, the rosier outlook is that the global economies are improving even slowly.

- January effect.
  The performance of January may determine how the entire year performs. I cannot find any rationale but it has been proven right statistically.

- Earnings period announced in Jan., April, July and Oct. would cause big swings in stocks when they have surprises. Earning revisions could be a good predictor.
  http://www.investopedia.com/terms/e/earningsseason.asp

Links
Presidential Cycle:
http://www.investopedia.com/articles/financial-theory/08/presidential-election-cycle.asp
Calendar-based market timing:
http://stock-chartist.com/2010/10/calendar-based-market-timing/
Calendar market timing for 2013:
http://www.investorecho.com/archives/8047

#Filler: Golden Gate

Just moments ago, my mail system demanded I sign in. I did—again and again—only to be asked to sign in yet again. Frustrated, I shut everything down and followed Gates' golden rule: *"If nothing works, just reboot."* So I powered everything off, said a little prayer, and turned it all back on. Miraculously, it worked. Thanks, Gates, for solving a problem you may have created.

What happened to basic quality control? In my day, people got fired for this kind of sloppiness. Today? Mediocrity seems to be the new norm.

#Filler: my friend's poem
My friend once wrote a poem in Chinese. Here's my translation:

- When you understand "everything is changing," you won't boast about your success—today's triumph can become tomorrow's burden.
- When you understand "everything is changing," you won't dwell in sadness—today's loss could become tomorrow's opportunity.
- When you understand "everything is changing," you'll stop reacting impulsively to daily ups and downs.

2   Summary

I made the following charts so it is easier to time the market by the calendar.

All dates are inclusive.

No.	Metric		Score
1	Seasonal	Nov. - April, Score = 1	
2	Best Month	Nov., Score = 1	
		Sep., Score = -1	
3	Best Days	Dec. 15 – Jan.15 Score = 1	
4	Presidential Cycle	Election Year, Score = 1	
		1st Year in Office, Score = -1	
		2nd year, Score = -1	
		3rd year, Score = 2	
5	Presidential[3]	Democratic = 1 Republican = -1	
6	Market Cycle	Early Recovery, Score = 3	
		Up, Score = 2	
		Peak, Score = 1	
7	SPY (Finviz.com)	SMA200% > 8%[2] Score = -1	
		SMA200% < 0 Score = -1	
		RSI(14) > 65% Score = -1	
		Grand Score	

Footnote.
1   Refer to the Market Cycle chapter on how I define phases of a cycle.
2   For simplicity, use Finviz.com. Enter SPY and you will find SMA200% and RSI(14) to predict whether the market is peaking and overbought.
3   I'm politically neutral. The selection is based on historical statistics.

Add up all the scores. The passing grade is 0. According to my table which is based on my personal selections/preferences, the market is favorable when the grand score is 1 or higher. I bet it is the first time you see such a scoring system for market timing.

Sectors for market cycle

Market Phase[1]	Favorable		Unfavorable
Early Recovery	Financial, Technology, Industrial		Energy, Telecom, Utilities
Up	Technology, Industrial		
Peak	Mineral, Health Care, Energy		
Bottom	Consumer Staples, Utilities		Consumer Discretionary, Technology, Industrial
Seasonal	**Favorable**		**Unfavorable**
Winter	Energy, Utilities		
End of year	QQQ, EWG		
Olympics	ETF for host country[2]		

Footnote.
1   Refer to the Market Cycle chapter on how I define phases of a cycle.
2   Buy it next year after the Olympics. It could be due to higher GDP or the publicity. However, be selective. Greece is too small a country to host an Olympics.

#Filler: The Tough, the Bad, and the Ugly Sectors
- Apparel has long been a brutal battleground (think Aeropostale).
- Mobile carriers endlessly match each other's family-plan deals—until coverage or hidden fees bite you.
- Bank CEOs who caused crises still pocket bonuses. (Enough said.)

Section V: Peaks and bottoms

It will be great when we can sell at peaks and buy at bottoms. It is not that easy. However, I try to find the common characteristics of peaks and bottoms. No tools can detect them. Otherwise, there would be no poor folks. The following are my suggestions.

1   Market peaks / bottoms

Summary by tables from my findings

The dates could be a little different from my similar tables as I use monthly data instead of daily data. The data are subject to my interpretations and the tables are used for illustration purposes only.

Table: Market Plunges

Market Plunge	Months (Peak to Bottom)	Loss	Annualized Loss
2000	17	56%	40%
2007	25	47%	23%
Average	21	51%	31%

Table: Vital Dates

Market Plunge	Peak	Bottom	Indicator Exit	Indicator Reentry
2000	08/28/00	09/20/02	10/30/00	05/26/03
2007	10/12/07	03/06/09	01/03/08	09/08/09

Most investors were fully invested in 2007 and 2008 and NOT fully invested in 2009. It proves the majority of us are performing worse than the market. If you followed the exit indicator and the reentry indicator, you should do far better than the average investor. A brief exit and reentry in the 2007 market cycle is skipped for simplicity (I call it a false signal).

Market plunges

The SMA-350 (Single Moving Average for 350 trade sessions) has detected the last two crashes (2000 and 2007) correctly leaving us a lot of time to prepare. It is based on the falling market, so it will detect the next market plunge. However, we may not be that lucky to have plenty of time to prepare for it (selling most of our positions) as in the last two (2000 and 2007).

Market peaks and bottoms

From the above table, the chart does not spot the peak and the bottom as expected. We would make far more money when selling at the peak and buying at the bottom. A dream perhaps?

SMA and/or RSI would confirm that the market is close to its peak or bottom. I gathered their values for the last two peaks and bottoms and I summarized them in this article. It is based on limited data and we treat the conclusions as nothing more than useful guidelines.

SMA, SMA% and RSI

SMA-20 (Single Moving Average for the last 20 trade days), SMA-50, SMA-200 and RSI(14) are the indicators I used. Look them up on Investopedia.com if you are not familiar with how they are used. Most are available in Finviz.com by specifying SPY as the stock symbol.

SMA percentages measure how far away is the market from their respective moving average. If the SPY's SMA-200 is 100 and the stock price is 200, the SMA-200% is 100% over the moving average. It would indicate that the market may be peaking.

SMA-200% = (Stock Price – SMA) / SMA
= (200 – 100) / 100 = 100%

RSI(14) measures whether the market is over or under bought using the last 14 trade sessions.

For detecting market crashes, I still prefer SMA-350. SMA-20 is good for predicting the short-term trend of a stock, but not for the entire market.

Bring Finviz.com up from your browser and enter SPY (or any market ETF representing the majority of your stocks). The SMA-n percentages and RSI(14) are displayed.

Misc.

Advance / Decline (AD or Buy/Sell ration). When it is below 1, be careful that the market could be near the top even if the S&P 500 index is rising. The theory is that fund managers (who drive the market) believe the market is risky, they want to unload the small stocks. They still want to keep or even add the investment on blue chips, which they are easier to unload when the market crashes. It indicates the market could be near the top. It is similar to (# of stocks making new heights) − (# of stocks making new lows). If it is positive and the market is rising, the market could be still fine.

The market could be heading up from the bottom as indicated by the following technical indicators.

- RSI(14) from SPY or RSP is less than 30%.
- AD is less than .2
- With the previous sessions mostly in red candles, the market changes to a long green candle.
- Both SMA-20 and SMA-50 for the market index are positive, and SMA-20 is more positive than SMA-50.

Findings

I include my findings in 3 sections: market timing for crashes, market timing for corrections and briefly on individual stocks, which have many other factors to consider.

I try to exit the market during market plunges (i.e., the stock price of SPY is below its SMA-350). My greed does not always allow me to do so entirely.

Market corrections provide opportunities to buy stocks. However, you need to accumulate cash in advance to take advantage of the temporary dips and prepare a list of stocks to buy at specified prices. For market plunges, we should not buy any stocks.

Market corrections of 5% happen about twice a year (or a 10% correction once a year), but its frequency varies. They are harder to detect, so do not leave the market totally. I prefer to keep less than 15% in cash to buy in the expected market dips. 2013 is a good year for stocks and in preparing for the corrections you could miss the opportunity of making more money.

Conclusion via a table

My test data are using SPY from 1-2000 to 2-2014. The following is from my own interpretation. Again, past information does not guarantee future performance. It just serves as a guideline.

	SMA-50	SMA-200	SMA-350	SMA50/ SMA200	RSI (14)
Market					
Peak		5%	9%	101%	65%
Bottom		-32%	-31%	78%	25%
Correction					
Peak	4%	6%	11%	102%	65%
Bottom	-5%	-6%	-7%	97%	26%
Stock					
Peak					70%
Bottom					30%

As explained, the market is plunging when the stock price of SPY is below its SMA-350 (i.e., the SMA-350% is negative). From my table, the market could be peaking when SMA-350 is 9% or above.

From the first glance, it is quite logical. At market peaks or temporary peaks, the SMA% is substantially over 0% and RSI(14) is far higher than the RSI(14) in the market bottoms.

Corrections are harder to determine. I have tested two times in different ways to determine corrections and the results are a little different.

The first method is to identify the peaks of the corrections and then get the averages of SMA-50, SMA-200%, SMA-350% and the RSI(14).

The second approach is more complicated and more subjective to describe here. The above table is a combination of the two approaches.

The market is not always rational. Today's market is influenced by the low interest rates.

What to act

Everyone wants to sell at the peak and buy at the bottom. However, these technical indicators and my interpretation may not always work.

When the market is peaking

To illustrate, when SMA-350 is over 9% (i.e., SPY's stock price is 9% over its SMA for the last 350 trade sessions) and/or RSI(14) is over 65%, it may indicate the market is peaking and overbought. I recommend:

- Accumulate cash but less than 15% of your portfolio. The actual percent depends on your risk tolerance. For those who do not care much about market fluctuations or do not have the time to trade stocks, do not play market timing on corrections.

- Sell the stocks that have appreciated enough to meet your objectives and/or their appreciation potentials are less than the average of your portfolio. Preferably, sell the stock with less tax implications (such as those qualifying for long term capital gain in your taxable accounts).

  Alternatively, buy one stock for every two stocks you sell when the peak drags on.

- Do not buy any new stocks with the above exception.

- Enforce stop loss that turns your sell orders to market orders when they fall below specific prices. Adjust the stop orders when the stocks appreciate (but do nothing when they depreciate).

My suggestion is using 5% stop loss and 10% stop loss for volatile stocks. To reduce excessive trading, you can use 10% and 15% instead. After the earnings announcement (available in Finviz), the stock would fluctuate far more than 5%, so adjust them before their earnings announcement dates.

When the market is bottoming

You want to reenter the market when the stock price for SPY (or other ETF simulating the market) is above the SMA-350. The following two suggestions when to reenter the market earlier. They are riskier but have better rewards if the guess is correct.

- Start to reenter the market when SMA-200% (the stock price is above the SMA-200) is positive.
- Start to reenter the market when SMA-350% is less than -31% and/or RSI(14) is less than 25%, it may indicate the market is bottoming and under-bought.

Do the following:
- Buy the stocks that have the best appreciation potential and most are fundamentally sound and beaten up badly by the general market. Alternatively, buy two stocks for every stock you sell.
- Do not sell any stocks with the above exception.
- You need to prepare a list of stocks to buy and at what prices when the market is plunging. If you do not have such a list, buy ETFs.

What to do in a market correction
It is very similar to market timing on crashes as above. However, I recommend keeping cash to less than 15% of your portfolio. Again, corrections are far harder to detect. 2013 has fewer and smaller corrections due to the excessive supply of money.

Stocks

Stocks are treated as overbought when the RSI(14) is over 70% and under-bought when it is below 30%; most stocks fluctuate more than the market. Some may use 65% for overbought and 35% for under-bought.

Depending on how long you usually keep a stock, you select the number of days in SMA. For example, if you keep most stocks for 200 days, use SMA-200. Buy when the range of its SMA-200% is ranging from 0 to 10% and the RSI is less than 60% as a rough guideline. Some stocks may just shoot up disregarding their fundamental and technical metrics. One's opinion. Selecting the SMA percent also depends on your risk tolerance. There are many other factors to consider on individual stocks such as a major lawsuit(s), losing/gaining market share... Again, use the above as a very rough guideline for the stocks.

Afterthoughts
- You will find many related articles on this topic by searching using Google.
- As of 3/5/2014, the market was supposed to be peaking as SMA-350% was 15% and RSI(14) was 73%. The historical data for these metrics can be shown on charts.
- Articles on market top.
  Business Insider.
  The flow to equity is a good contrary indicator (the more money goes to equity funds by retail investors, the more chance the market will plunge).
  http://www.businessinsider.com/signs-this-is-not-a-market-peak-2013-12
  The 15 signs.
  http://theeconomiccollapseblog.com/archives/15-signs-that-we-are-near-the-peak-of-an-absolutely-massive-stock-market-bubble

2   Peaking and Overbought

This chapter is an extension of the last one. The following indicators are not very reliable and they should be used as secondary indicators. However, exiting from the peak could make you more money if the signal is correct. When the price is 9% over the simple moving average SMA-350, the market may be peaking. This ratio is defined by:

(Price – Moving Average) / Moving Average.

When the RSI(14) is over 65%, the market could be overbought (i.e., highly valued). This ratio can be found in Finviz.com with SPY or another ETF that represents the market as the stock symbol. It is defined as:

RSI = 100 - 100/(1 + RS)

where RS = Average of x days' up closes / Average of x sessions RSI(14) is the relative strength index using the last 14 trade sessions.

The reentry point is less than -31% for the SMA-350 ratio and less than 25% for the RSI(14). Again, they are used for a guideline only.

Suggested Actions

Peaking and overbought conditions indicate the market is overvalued. My suggestion is not to sell all positions except those stocks that are overvalued or have met your objectives. Place stop orders to protect profits. I recommend 5% below the current price and 10% for volatile stocks (10% and 15% are fine in today's volatile market). When the stock price rises, change the stop orders accordingly. When the stock is sold, accumulate cash until these conditions change.

I recommend using the cash to buy CDs and short-term, bonds that are investment grade. Save some cash to buy contra ETFs when the market is plunging. 2008 was not a good year for bonds, but 2009 was. Based on this, I would sell the bonds when the market is crashing. Investing is not a 100% sure thing. These are my recommendations and you need to modify the plan according to your risk tolerance.

3   Design a test for market peaks/bottoms

This article describes how to set up a test for the last article on detecting market peaks/bottoms by using SMA and RSI. There is no need to understand how I derived the results and it could serve as a model for designing a test for another strategy.

Objective
To find out any common values of SMA and RSI when the market plunges, corrects or surges.

The data for this test are obtained from Yahoo!Finance and/or charts available from many other free sites.

How to get data

From Yahoo!Finance, enter SPY for the stock. Select historical prices from 1/3/96 to 2/5/14 in my example. Use the prices adjusted for splits and dividends; in this case it may not make any difference. Load it to Excel. Sort the date in the ascending order. Delete the columns I do not need.

Adjusted Close Price is mostly the one you want to use for testing to compensate for the split and dividend.
https://help.yahoo.com/kb/finance/SLN2311.html?impressions=true

Most historical databases do not include dividends but handle splits. Hence, we have to adjust accordingly. Add the dividend rate (about 1.75%) to the annualized return rate where appropriate.

Get critical dates

I limited my test data to the last two crashes (2000 and 2007). The test data before 2000 may not reflect today's market. Here are the critical dates from my other book.

Table: Vital Dates

Market Plunge	Peak	Bottom	Indicator Exit	Indicator Reenter
2000	08/28/00	09/20/02	10/30/00	05/26/03

2007	10/12/07	03/06/09	01/03/08	09/08/09

Get statistics on previous peaks and bottoms

To illustrate, the peak in 2000 is 08/28/00, calculate the SMA-200, SMA-350, SMA-50 and SM50/SMA200 for this date. Actually, I included 4 days before and 4 days after and averaged all the mentioned parameters for a total of 9 days. Try to automate this procedure as much as possible.

Repeat the above for 2007. Average the parameters in the two market plunges.

Repeat the same for the two market bottoms.

RSI(14)

There is too much logic to calculate this indicator. I used the RSI from charts for the critical dates. Select RSI in the chart.

Filler: OTC, cars and filthy rich in 5 seconds

OTC, over-the-counter stocks, are risky as many do not have information required by SEC and the major exchanges. They are traded over the counter, OTC. They cannot be shorted (and most likely you do not want to do so even if it was allowed). Pier 1, Ford, American Airlines and many others were all penny stocks.

Expect one winner for several losers. However, the total profit could outpace the total loss if the strategy is properly implemented.

Filler: Advances in cars
I have not used cruise control even ONCE. I could be the exception. The more complex the car, the more chance it breaks down.

A few years ago, I got an on-line statement from my broker saying I had over 10M. I took a screenshot. When I logged off and logged on again, my millions were gone and so were many better

things in life I planned to buy. What a tough life! I try to say the car computer could break down too and it may cause lives.

4   Market peak example

It is hard to determine market peaks and bottoms. Otherwise, there would be no poor folks. Based on data from 7/4/2017, I tried to predict (again predict) whether the market is peaking. From my previous findings:

Table: Market Plunges

Market Plunge	Months (Peak to Bottom)	Loss	Annualized Loss
2000	17	56%	40%
2007	25	47%	23%
Average	21	51%	31%

Table: Vital Dates

Market Plunge	Peak	Bottom	Indicator Exit	Indicator Reentry
2000	08/28/00	09/20/02	10/30/00	05/26/03
2007	10/12/07	03/06/09	01/03/08	09/08/09

My test data uses the SPY from 1-2000 to 2-2014 to get the averages of the peaks. The following is from my own interpretation. Again, past information does not guarantee future performance. It just serves as a guideline.

	SMA-50	SMA-200	SMA-350	SMA50/ SMA200	RSI (14)
Market (SPY)					
Peak (avg.)		5%	9%	101%	65%
7/4/2017	0%	6%	10%	N/A	50%

Both SMA-200% and SMA-350% are on par with the averages of the previous two market peaks. RSI(14) shows the market is overbought but it is 15% less than the average. I missed some parameters such as P/E. The P/E as of 7/4/17 is 25.69 and is about 71% more expensive assuming the average is 15. The average of 11 stocks from Fidelity's best sector list increased by only 0.35% for last month. So, it is not a good sign.

Fundamental metrics (07/20/2017)

	L.T. Avg.	7/20/ 17	High by[1]	Min	On	Max	On
P/E[2]	15.66	26.17	67%	5.31	12-1917	123.73	05-2017
Shiller P/E[2]	16.76	30.12	80%	4.78	12-1920	44.19	12-1999
P/Sales[2]	1.45	2.15	48%	0.8	03-2009	2.15	07-2017
P/Book[2]	2.75	3.22	17%	4.78	12-1920	44.19	12-1999

[1] High by = (Current – Mean) /Mean

[2] From http://www.multpl.com/.

The market is fundamentally overvalued as indicated in 07/04/2017.

The transport index (DJT) could be an indicator too. It loses its luster due to web sales not depending on rails and trucks.
Read articles on the current market such as this one.
https://www.marketwatch.com/story/the-biggest-problem-in-the-stock-market-bullishness-is-clouding-investors-thinking-2020-08-27?mod=home-page

Section VI: Market timing experiences

Overview
The following insights reflect real-world market behavior versus beginning-of-year forecasts. Actual performance data from **RSP**—an equal-weighted S&P 500 ETF—illustrates how market timing, while valuable, remains inherently uncertain. Always align your strategy with your **risk tolerance** and **consult a financial advisor** before making significant investment decisions.

Year	RSP	Year	RSP

2020	10%	2023	12%
2021	30%	2024	11%
2022	-13%	Avg: 2020-2024	**10%**

1 Market timing: 2008-2015

I used Fidelity's charting tools to generate a **350-day Simple Moving Average (SMA)** on SPY (a proxy for the S&P 500) from **Dec. 2008 to Dec. 2015**. Here's what I observed:

- From 2000 to 2009, my SMA-350 model produced only **one false signal**.
- Between 2010 and 2015, **false signals increased**, possibly due to more investors following technical indicators— leading to greater volatility.

While using **SMA-400** could reduce false alarms, I chose to stick with SMA-350 for its earlier warnings, especially anticipating possible interest rate hikes in 2016.

By **August 2015**, my cash allocation was around **50%**, although my chart suggested going 100% cash. I held back, influenced by greed.

Even as of **Dec. 1, 2015**, with SPY above the SMA-350, I maintained a conservative position. Ultimately, **risk tolerance** determines how much cash to hold. I later planned to reduce cash after executing my year-end "loser strategy."

2 Market timing: 2021

As of early 2021, the market was hitting new highs. Analysts were split—some predicted a crash, others expected continued growth. The market was fundamentally **overvalued**, yet technically **strong**, due to massive cash injections from the Fed.

Technical Indicators (SPY via Finviz.com)
- **Death Cross**: No
- **SMA-350**: Price above = Pass
- **RSI(14)**: 61 = Pass
- **Duration since last bear market**: 10 years = Fail

Fundamental Valuation Metrics
(All were significantly overvalued and thus failed.)
- **P/E**: 25.4 vs avg <15.7 → Fail
- **Shiller P/E**: 33.5 vs avg <16.6 → Fail
- **P/B**: 3.52 vs avg <2.78 → Fail

- **P/S**: 2.33 vs avg <1.5 → Fail

Macro Factors

- **Oil Price**: $70 – Pass
- **T-Bill rates (1m, 3m, 30y)**: Under 5% – Pass
- **Corporate Debt/GDP**: 45% – Fail
- **USD Strength**: Weak – Fail
- **Gold Price**: High – Fail
- **Bubble Indicators**: Several – Fail
- **Expert Sentiment**: Neutral to fearful – Caution
- **Political Risks (e.g., trade war)** – Fail

Overall Assessment: The market looked risky, especially based on fundamentals.

Tip: SPY is market cap-weighted and heavily skewed toward FAANG stocks. Consider ETFs with broader or equal-weight exposure for better market representation.

A table summarizing the above

P/B[3]	<2.78	3.52	High by 27%. Fail.
P/S[3]	<1.50	2.33	High by 55%. Fail.
Oil price	30-100	70.71	Pass
Interest rate[6] T-Bill 1 months[7]	<5	2.05	Pass
T-Bill 3 months[7]	Yield	2.18	
T-Bill 30 years[7]	Curve	3.20	Pass
Flow to Equity[4]		-3.371M	Fail
Flow to bond[4]		7.206M	
Corporate debt/GDP[8]	<40	45%	High by 13%. Fail.
USD[5]		Strong	Fail
Gold		High	Fail
Bubble		Several	Fail
Market experts		Fear long term	Neutral
Politics		Trump	Fail
Misc.		Trade war	Fail
		Overall	**Fail**

[1] This is the market timing technique without using a chart.
[2] I tried to use SMA-400% to reduce false signals without success.
[3] Get it from http://www.multpl.com/. Same as CAPE.

[4] Get it from https://www.ici.org/research/stats. It is based on 09-12-18. "Flow to Equity" is based on domestic ETF estimates. Treat it as two phases in moving to equity. First phase of moving excessively to equity indicates the market is peaking. The second phase indicates the market is plunging when the flow of equity is excessively negative.

[5] Global corporations will suffer in profits converted back to USD and hard to sell to foreign countries.

[4] Get it from the above link.

[6] Rising interest is bad for corporations and high-ticket products, but good for lenders.

[7] Get it from https://www.treasury.gov/resource-center/data-chart-center/interest-rates/Pages/TextView.aspx?data=yield based on 09/21/18

[8] With the low interest rate, it may not be that critical. Corporations take advantage of the low interest rate.

Here is a list of sites for charts.
https://www.stocktrader.com/2013/12/10/best-free-stock-chart-websites/
These are the three sites I use a lot: Fidelity (customers only), StockCharts and Finviz.com (missing some metrics).

As stated before, SPY may not be the best to represent the market. I prefer an ETF for 1,000 stocks and weigh the stocks evenly (i.e., not according to the market cap). Google "market timing 2020 (or current year)" for more expert info. Here is one.

Mid-Year (2020) Update

Despite a sluggish economy, the market surged due to the Fed's aggressive quantitative easing (QE). The **debt-to-GDP** ratio reached levels last seen before the 2000 crash.

- **NASDAQ (QQQ)** outperformed YTD.
- I used **trailing stops, contra ETFs**, and **gold miners** as hedges.
- **Oil ETFs underperformed**.
- I held **precious metals and cash** as protection.

Warning: If the U.S. dollar loses reserve currency status, expect **high inflation** and possibly a prolonged **depression**. In that case, favor hard assets (real estate, gold) and profitable companies over bonds or CDs.

3   Market timing: early 2022

This article was written in **March 2022** and updated in **May**.
- My **Simple Market Timing** strategy gave an exit signal on **March 20, 2022**.
- Although I didn't fully exit, the strategy was validated.

Bearish Indicators
- **VIX**: 20% above average
- **Shiller P/E**: 33% vs 20-year avg of 26%
- **Buffett Indicator (Market Cap/GDP)**: 180% vs benchmark 75%

I began:
- Reducing contra ETFs
- Trading gold, precious metals, and oil (USO)
- Accumulating cash in anticipation of recovery

➤ Watch for **Golden Cross** and **SMA-350** signals before re-entering. Consider VTI (total market ETF) or select undervalued stocks.

4   Market timing: 2023

Written in **February 2023** after attending a 3-hour Yahoo!Finance forum.
Two opposing camps emerged:
- **Soft landing** with mild recession
- **Hard landing** and significant downturn

One analyst recommended shifting from **defensive sectors** (e.g., Utilities, Staples) to **beaten-down ones** (e.g., Tech, Pharma). I preferred using **SMA-50** to confirm uptrends before buying.

Historically, U.S. markets have **not fallen in a pre-election year** since WWII—this trend held in 2023.

In early 2023, **AI-related stocks** (e.g., NVDA, MSFT) surged. NVDA was up 40%, MSFT 15% in one month. However, **China's DeepSeek AI** could disrupt this growth story by **January 2025**.

Update: March 2025
2024 was a strong year, largely fueled by AI.
2025, however, has started poorly—likely due to **tariff-related disruptions**. NVDA could be my largest stocks by percentage have been profiting with my utility stocks NRG and VST. AMD and GOOG are not faring well.

Links
How to invest in 2023's recession
https://www.youtube.com/watch?v=ALjWkfJjGUA

Section VII: Miscellaneous

1   A sideways market

The market moves up or down. Usually, it dances sideways when switching from one trend to the other. When it moves down, it moves at a faster speed. When the volume is unusually low, it could be a hint that the market is changing direction on me.

Market movements could be predicted by moving averages (30-days moving average is one for dips and 52 weeks for plunges for example). When it moves above the average line, most likely it will move up and vice versa.

For volatile markets, the last time it peaks and the last time it bottoms are termed as **resistance lines and support lines** respectively. In theory and theory only, a sideways market never breaks out from these two lines. It is a prediction only and many other factors should be considered. Even with all the right educated guesses, the market is not always rational.

Take advantage of the sideways movements by buying at small dips (the support line) and selling at small peaks (the resistance line).

You can take advantage of market timing by not holding a stock forever and by buying and selling the same stock or an ETF. I believe the 'buy-and-hold' idea has been dead since 2000. I cannot find too many articles praising this strategy with data after 2000.

Market plunges are usually fast and steep.

2015 Update. From my memory the last time we had a down year in a year before the election year was 1939, the start of WW2. Even 2007 was an up year. I had posted this info for 2015 even during the fierce correction in August, 2015. Adding the 1.9% dividend, the market beats the one-year CD by a good margin in 2015. To profit in this market, buy at temporary dips and sell at temporary surges.

Links

Resistance line and support line:
http://en.wikipedia.org/wiki/Support_and_resistance

Profit in bull, bear, and sideways markets

You don't need expert-level investing knowledge to profit in all three market conditions. You only need a few smart strategies and the discipline to follow them.

Bull Markets
- Use **momentum and breakout strategies**
- Focus on **growth stocks**
- Employ **trend-following techniques**
- Use **leverage** cautiously
- Protect gains with **stop-loss and trailing stops**

Bear Markets
- Shift to **consumer staples, CDs, contra ETFs**, and **precious metals**
- **Short-selling** can also be effective
- Practice **tight risk management**
- Accumulate cash and be ready to reenter when recovery begins

Sideways Markets
- Use **range-bound strategies**:
    - Trade support/resistance levels
    - Consider options (e.g., **straddles/strangles**)
    - Use **mean-reversion** techniques
- Begin rotating out of high-risk positions as the market transitions to bear territory

A simple method to identify a **sideways market** is when the price frequently crosses the **350-day SMA** without direction—indicating choppy, indecisive action.

2   Market timing by asset class

There are two main trading strategies for different asset classes:

1. **Buy High, Sell Higher**
   This is a **momentum** strategy. You ride the upward wave and sell quickly—typically within a few weeks or months. Momentum can reverse sharply, so holding periods are usually short. In my momentum portfolio, most stocks are held for less than a month.

2. **Buy Low, Sell High**
   This is a **value** strategy. You buy when an asset class is out of favor but fundamentally undervalued. This approach requires more patience, often holding for 6 months or longer, waiting for market sentiment to catch up to intrinsic value.

Predicting tops and bottoms precisely is nearly impossible. However, I've often seen **momentum lead early,** followed by **value** opportunities later in the cycle. The holding periods above are only general suggestions.

Enhancing Success with Technical Analysis
Technical analysis can improve your entry and exit timing. A simple starting point is the **50-day moving average** (i.e., 50 trading sessions). A basic rule of thumb:

- **Buy** when price moves above the moving average.
- **Sell** when it drops below.

You can experiment with shorter (20-day) or longer periods, as well as with exponential moving averages. Many tools, including **Finviz.com**, offer these indicators without requiring advanced charting.

There's always a tradeoff between acting **too frequently** (overtrading) and **reacting too late**. Also, different asset classes and individual stocks vary in volatility—adjust your strategy accordingly.

Applying to Different Assets (Gold as an Example)

No one can predict the exact top of an asset like gold. Suppose you buy gold at $1,000 and sell at $1,600—you've done well, even if gold later reaches $1,800.

To analyze gold technically, trade **GLD**, the gold ETF, rather than physical coins. Use **trailing stops** to protect profits—adjust them upward as prices rise.

My Experience with Gold

Years ago, I bought gold coins at ~$400. For decades, gold prices were flat. I sold some at $800 (100% return), but it likely didn't beat inflation. If I'd invested in stocks instead, the **total return** (including dividends) would've been significantly higher.

Selling more coins at $1,000 seemed wise at the time, but gold later hit $1,800. This illustrates how **human psychology** often prevents us from holding through peaks. We can't predict exact tops.

Also, trading physical gold involves high **commissions and spreads**. Local shops are safer, but watch IRS reporting rules based on sale amount.

Links

Disadvantages of gold ETFs:
https://www.youtube.com/watch?v=wMxj6iB92ZA

#Filler: Boring but Effective

When markets get risky, some investors refuse to hold cash—claiming it's just too boring.

If that's your logic, try this: toss a gold coin into the ocean every 15 minutes. You'll definitely draw a crowd—maybe a diver, maybe a cop, or maybe just someone dialing the nearest mental hospital.

Either way, you won't be bored... and you'll probably make the 6 o'clock news.

But if you'd rather keep your wealth *and* your sanity, maybe holding cash isn't so boring after all.

3   My predictions – what worked and what didn't

I've read books by authors who claimed they predicted the 2007 housing crash. Whether those calls were made **before or after** the fact is unclear. Some of these same authors also predicted another crash after 2008—which never came. If you had followed their advice to move all assets into cash, you would have missed the **strongest market recovery** from 2009 onward.

Key Lessons
- A single correct call doesn't ensure future success.
- Even bestselling authors can be **one-hit wonders**—some admit it, others don't.
- The economy doesn't always reflect the market. For example, **quantitative easing (QE)** lifted markets even as the economy lagged.

I had my best year in **2009**, recovering much of the 2007–08 loss. However, I turned overly conservative afterward.

This chapter is meant for **education**, not to validate every prediction. The goal is simple: **If our educated guesses are right more than 50% of the time, we can still profit.**

All investing is built on **informed predictions**. Accept that some will fail. Learn from both successes and mistakes—but recognize when outcomes are influenced by irrational markets or sheer luck.

Correct or Nearly Correct Predictions
- **2000**: Moved from tech to traditional sectors before the dot-com crash. Moving to cash or contra ETFs would've been better, but they weren't widely available then.
- **2003**: Re-entered stocks during early recovery.
- **2009**: Entered early and had my best return ever, even using (not recommended) a credit line.
- **2011–2012**: Forecasts for both years were close to reality.
- **April 2012 Correction**: Reasonably accurate.
- **June 2013 Correction**: Predicted a 10% dip, but market corrected only ~6%.

- **Stock picks**: My scoring system outperformed the market over the test period. For instance, I recommended Apple at $390.50 (pre-split) in May 2013.

Incorrect Predictions

- **2008 Crash**: Overconfidence from energy stock gains blinded me to broader economic risks. I ignored my own technical signals. A reminder of why systems matter more than recent wins.
- **Q1 2013 Correction**: Didn't happen—likely due to aggressive monetary stimulus. I held too much cash and missed gains. A case of "winning battles, losing the war."
- **Poor stock picks**: At times, I ignored my own advice and paid for it.

The Outlook for Future Predictions

The charting technique outlined in *Spotting Big Plunges*—especially the use of **moving averages**—worked well from **2000 to 2015**. It should continue to work, though future downturns may unfold faster, leaving **less reaction time**. In 2025, the market is not rational – Trump's words could change the entire market outlook. We need to concern with our huge national debt.

Summary

It's not about how often you predict correctly—it's about what you **learn** from each prediction. Every investment decision is a prediction. Some work. Some don't.

- **Diversify** to manage risk.
- **Learn** from your outcomes—good or bad.
- Focus on **systems**, not feelings or headlines.

#Filler: Street Wisdom on Market Crashes

Here are some golden rules about market plunges—passed down from seasoned investors (and a few bruised ones):

Rule #1: Anything can go wrong—because the market rarely acts rationally.
Rule #2: Markets tend to fall three times faster than they rise. Panic moves quicker than optimism.
Rule #3: A 50% loss requires a 100% gain just to break even. Think

about that before holding blindly.

Rule #4: The simpler the game seems, the fewer players are willing to stick around—until it's too late.

Rule #5: Retail investors often buy near the top, driven by greed and FOMO.

Rule #6: They also sell at the bottom, paralyzed by fear that the market will never recover. (Spoiler: it always does.)

Timing may not be everything—but panic is never a plan.

Fidelity's insight

Click on "News & Research" and then "Stock Market & Sector Performance" for Equity Market Commentary. The advantage is that Fidelity does not require paid subscriptions to see the entire article.

4   Reasons for the coming market crash (e.g. 2021-22)

This section is specific to 2021–2022 but offers lessons that may apply in the future. For several years, traditional predictors have failed—primarily due to excessive money supply, which has disconnected the stock market from the real economy. But this disconnect can't last forever. When liquidity dries up, the market and economy will realign.

The sharp recovery after the 2007–2008 crash was driven by aggressive money printing. The same pattern repeated in 2020, fueling asset inflation, easy credit, buyouts, and margin-fueled speculation—a textbook case of supply and demand distortion.

While markets typically perform well in pre-election years (e.g., 2007, 2019), **2021 posed significant risks**. As of early 2021, the fundamentals were weak, even if technicals remained strong. When both align negatively, it's time to exit the market—use the simple timing methods described in this book.

Positive Signs
- The COVID-19 pandemic was receding in impact.
- The economy was recovering, albeit unevenly.
- Energy prices were rebounding—positive for the sector.

- Near-zero interest rates boosted housing, corporate buybacks, and investment.

Warning Signs
- One of the longest bull markets in history.
- High unemployment and long-term damage to small businesses.
- Historically high margin debt.
- Limited tools left for the Fed to respond to future crises.
- National debt and unfunded obligations are rising sharply.
- Foreign buyers of U.S. debt are decreasing; the Fed is funding deficits via money printing.
- Many retailers were insolvent or nearing bankruptcy.
- The U.S. dollar weakened, threatening its reserve currency status.
- Inflation pressures were building.

Summary
By 2021, markets were dangerously inflated. Fueled by cheap money and speculative demand, they detached from economic fundamentals. That's a red flag—**be conservative when markets defy gravity**.

5   A simple but risky strategy for market timing

Refer to the "Simplest Market Timing" method in this book. When the indicators signal a downturn, take defensive actions based on your risk tolerance:
- Move to cash
- Buy contra ETFs
- Reduce exposure to risky sectors

Recommended ETFs
- **SPY** – S&P 500 ETF (for general market exposure)
- **PSQ** – Inverse NASDAQ ETF (targets tech sector declines)
- **SEF** – Inverse financial ETF (targets banks and financials)
- **GLD** – Gold ETF (for safety in downturns)
- **Money Market / CDs** – For capital preservation

Strategy Insights
- **Contra ETFs** perform well in bear markets by betting against specific sectors.
- **Gold (GLD)** typically outperforms in recessions, especially when the U.S. dollar weakens. Hold 2–10% of your portfolio in gold depending on your risk profile.
- **Money market funds/CDs** are best for conservative investors seeking safety during volatility.

While the method produced only one false signal from 2000 to 2010, there have been more false alarms since 2010. However, these rarely result in significant losses—especially if you avoid leveraged or inverse products.

After a Crash
When indicators signal recovery:
- **Sell contra ETFs**
- **Buy SPY or value ETFs**
- Gradually shift into well-researched value stocks
- Use **stop-loss orders** to protect gains

As always, consult a financial advisor. Your strategy should match your personal financial goals and risk tolerance.

6   Navigate in a stormy market (e.g., 2024 outlook)

Caution First
As of 2024, if you followed the book's advice that "since WWII, the market tends to rise in the year before an election," you would have performed well so far. But the risks remain elevated due to:
1. Excessive money printing
2. Geopolitical threats (e.g., rising tensions with China)

For Conservative Investors
- Stick with **money market funds, CDs, and short-term bond funds**.
- Consider **laddering CDs**, especially when rates are high (e.g., 8%+).

- Invest in **long-term CDs** only if rates peak and you're not planning to reenter stocks soon.

For Moderate and Aggressive Investors
- Focus on **value stocks** with:
    - Low debt
    - Minimal insider selling (check via Finviz.com)
- Use **stop-loss** and **trailing stop orders**:
    - For low-volatility stocks: ~5%
    - For volatile ones: ~10%
- Revisit stop levels weekly, or use automated tools that suggest better levels based on resistance.

Apply the **same stop strategy to momentum trades**, and keep holding periods short (e.g., one month).

Use Market Timing
- Exit the market based on simple signals outlined in this book.
- Reenter when conditions improve—don't ignore **false signals**, as they often result in minimal impact apart from taxes.

While out of the market, **park your capital** in safe instruments like CDs or short-term bond funds.
Aggressive traders may:
- Buy **contra ETFs**
- **Short stocks**, using stop-losses for protection

Stay informed through credible financial sources (e.g., Fidelity) and YouTube. Expect conflicting opinions—use them for perspective, not absolute direction.

*** Bonus: Economy / Strategies

By the time you read this book, the current events may not be that current. Use the lessons to predict the future events.

1   Economy theories

I read this article predicting the "End of the economic cycle".
https://seekingalpha.com/article/4253126-weighing-week-ahead-near-end-economic-cycle?v=1554645177&comments=show

Why most market predictions by economists are wrong

It is interesting. The market cycle usually is 6 months ahead of the economic cycle. Based on this, the 'end' argument does not hold true. However, as of 4/09/2019, the market fundamentals are bad. I would move more to CDs after the settling of the trade war with China. To be warned, all markets are different.

I have about 10 hints for a potential market crash. The most deciding factor for me is the SMA, Simple Moving Average. When it turns negative, it is time to exit the market. The number of days in SMA depends on your risk tolerance. It is described in my book "Profit from coming market crash". SMA does not pinpoint the market peaks / bottoms as it depends on past data.

Most economists are wrong in predicting the market. The former Fed chairman said the economy was great and after a few months in 2008 the market crashed. There are many other factors such as politics and geopolitics. To illustrate, if there is a major war in the Middle East, the market would tank no matter how good the economy is.

The good job report is good for the economy as it would reduce the chance of a recession. However, if it is too good, the Fed would raise interest rates to cool down the over-heated economy and hence it would reduce corporate profits. Historically the market usually responds unfavorably to extreme low unemployment reports.

The job report on April, 2019 is fine for both the economy and the stock market. However, mathematically incorrect, it is close to a practical zero unemployment.

Grouping world's economies

The world's leading economies are US/EU (with Canada and Australia) and the challengers are Japan, S. Korea and China in the last two decades. The first group's success is due to technology starting in the Industrial Revolution in Britain. The U.S. joined the group after WW2 when Europe was destroyed.

Eliminating resource-rich countries and small countries, we have about 25 countries leading the global economies. There are no strict rules on how to define a leading country. Most use GDP. I use GDP per capita adjusted for purchase power. U.S.'s GNP is higher than GDP as she owns a lot of foreign investments. China may not be counted as one by GDP per capita alone. However, China is the #2 economy due to its huge population and will be within the coming decade I expect.

The first group is declining slowly and is being replaced by the second group. It will take decades to be totally replaced judging from the decline of Spain and Italy which is described next.

In 1850s, Spain and Italy were the richest countries with the 'loots' from South American and other colonies. When the country is rich, the citizens want to enjoy life by asking for higher salaries, more vacation days, better social welfare, more protection for the workers and the environment. Hence, they lack the incentive to work harder and their products are less competitive. Are the U.S. and the EU countries repeating history?

The other factor is population size. Populations in most of the mentioned countries are shrinking. Aging population makes the problem worse. You need more educated and productive citizens. They solve part of the problem by immigration. EU is learning the hard way from many incidents caused by terrorists from immigration. The U.S. needs to immigrate top scientists to make us more competitive and the workers who are taking farm jobs and jobs not wanted by the social welfare recipients.

Most of these countries are borrowing heavily – a common trick by politicians in buying votes. It solves the current problems and buys some votes, but it will be a big burden for next generations. Watch out when the national debt is about twice the GDP. Japan has the lost decades. We and many EU countries have not learned from Japan. China has the same problem now. In addition, China's population has been surprisingly reduced even with the new two-child policy.

Most countries not included in the two groups will remain poor for decades to come. Many countries in Africa and S. America have high fertility rates. They may consume all the limited resources.

Most countries in the second group of the advanced economies are influenced by Confucius who teaches them to serve man and their family (actually the emperor to be precise). Confucius teaches them to be frugal (saving money for investing) and better educated for innovation.

It could be the climate too. Folks in the north have to work hard to prepare and save food for the winter. In warm climates, folks are lazier as described in my Coconut Theory. It does not explain why Australians are wealthy.

Another factor is life style. Many countries not included in the two group enjoy their life style by not chasing material stuff. They are happy by singing and dancing without fancy smart phones. Lack of consumption of fancy products would not make them an advanced economy. Good or bad? You decide. That's one reason Mao's era was backward as they're not chasing satisfaction from these consumers' products.

Globalization

During Reagan's era, globalization was preached and practiced. You do not want to grow sugar cane in Alaska. With the reduced cost of transportation and cheap labor in many countries, globalization has more benefits than drawbacks.

Many of our global companies have been making profits and GM may be saved from the second bankruptcy with the profits from China. We can find many U.S. fast food chains, U.S. movies and music and retail stores all over the world even in China.

The drawbacks are numerous. One major one is our huge trade deficit with China as she becomes the manufacturing capital of the world. As a result we have been losing a lot of factory jobs. The major drawbacks in China are both the air and water pollution. The other drawbacks are the lack of selection of products as price always favors over value for most consumers.

Both countries are addressing the problems. China will be more aligned with EU if she is being punished by us. China will buy more jets from Airbus than Boeing.

GDP and global trades

GDP normally means GDP growth after inflation.

Inflation is important. If the inflation is 10%, the GDP of 10 without including inflation is actually GDP of 0.

If the GDP is calculated in the U.S. currency, the currency conversion rate is important.

The average GDP for developing countries is about 5.5% and that for developed countries like the U.S. is about 3%.

China was about 6.2% in 2018. It is not a fully developed country. It used to be around 10 digits for many years after joining WTO in 2001. It is down from 2017's 6.9%. I predict it will be down below 6% if the trade war with the U.S. continues.

WTO rules have not been enforced fully on China esp. on subsidies and exporting their excessive capacity (product dumping for some). Most countries subsidized in some of their industries. Product dumping will in theory benefit the importing countries. We make sure that they will not raise prices after the local competitors have been driven out of business. Microsoft did dump their Office products one time. In addition, Microsoft and Apple copied many ideas from PARC.

China's GDP depends on the GDPs reported from the provinces. Most likely most provinces over-reported their GDPs.

Absolute GDP takes a back seat to GDP growth. The Debt / Absolute GDP ratio is important. Absolute GDP per capita is important when a living standard is concerned.

China is #1 in global trade. China owns less farm land and many natural resources such as oil per capita. China can use her trading position for political gains. During the current trade war with the U.S., Australia who is siding with the U.S. would lose a lot of Australia imports to China.

Filler: Golden Gate

Just minutes ago, my mail system asked me to sign in. I did and repeatedly they asked me to sign in again and again. I closed down everything and followed Gates' golden rule: If everything does not work, just power down everything and power it up again. I did this and prayed too. It works. Thanks Gates for fixing my problem.

There is NO one doing BASIC quality control. If it happened in my generation, many guys would be fired. Mediocrity is the new norm?

2   Falling oil price

When oil price is down below $30, I believe it is a buy to the investors. 3/2020 is the second chance after 1/2016. It may happen again in 2021. We had a chance to buy when the oil price fell almost to zero. The long-term future of oil is not that good. Many countries are switch to green energies. However, it is far less polluting than coal. In Dec. 2020, I found many oil companies had attractive forward P/Es.

The cost of the oil depends on the following factors:

- The ease of drilling. The production cost for most oil ranges from $2 to $20. Most drillers are not profitable when the oil price per barrel is below $50. Most cheap oils (close to the earth surface) have gone except in Saudi Arabia.
- The quality of oil. Most of Saudi Arabia's oil are good quality while Venezuela's oil is heavy and very expensive to refine.
- Transportation. It is least expensive if it is close to the customer. Venezuela has a long way to transport except the U.S.A.
- Competition of shale energy and now the reduced cost of green energy such as solar and wind.

High oil reserve (Venezuela is among one of them) does not mean high production due to the above factors.

#Fillers: I wish I have a time machine

After collecting bottles for money, an old lady ordered a bowl of plain rice and ate by herself. I wish I could have ordered a meat dish for her as I was 'ashamed' of being generous.

A well-dressed gentleman offered his just-bought hamburger to a beggar. The beggar refused and asked for money instead – most likely he needed the money to buy liquor. A tale of two citizens.

During a lunch with my fellow tourists, a beautiful girl danced for our entertainment. I did not offer her anything and it had been bothering me for years.

During college, my housemates asked me to apply for food stamps. I had used only a few stamps then as I did not cook. I feel ashamed as this is my only time to collect social welfare. We have regrets in life and we can only bring them to our graves.

The oil prices for the last 10 years from Nasdaq.com:

Home > Markets > Commodities > Crude Oil Brent

Crude Oil Brent

Latest Price & Chart for Crude Oil Brent

End of day Commodity Futures Price Quotes for Crude Oil Brent

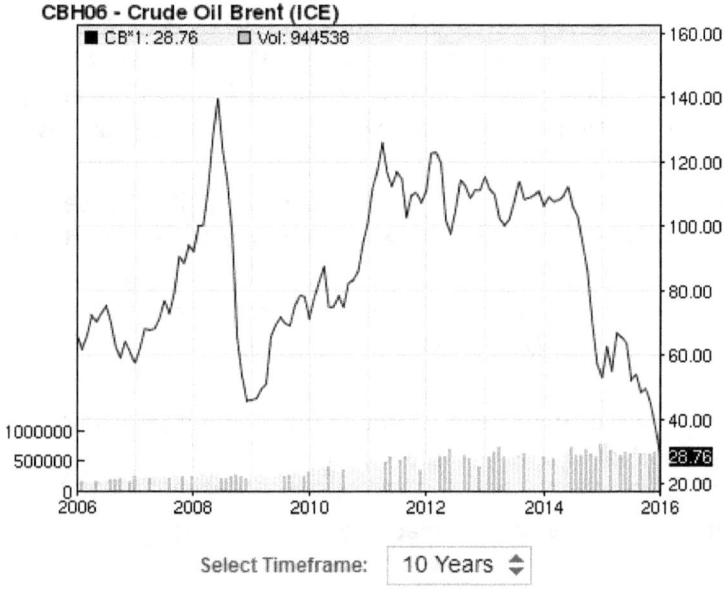

Crude Oil Brent Related ETFs: BNO

My predictions

Prediction #1. For the year, it will be in $25 to $40 per barrel. Personally I will not wait for a $25 rate as it may never materialize.

Reasons:

- Global economies have not recovered yet.

- Iran's oil will add more supply.
- OPEC and Russia cannot trim supply as their economies depend on oil export.

Prediction #2. For years later, it will return to $50 per barrel and be on its way to $100.

Reasons:

- Global economies will recover (they always do). But I do not know when that will happen.
- OPEC will trim their supply.
- Supply will be reduced due to the current cut back on drilling and exploration.
- Global population growth.
- Inflation (about 3% per year).
- Historical prices. Recently we had oil prices below $30 and then it went up to $140. Adjusted for inflation, the current price is even far less than $30.
- As a rough estimate (depending on individual oil fields), it takes about $50 to extract, market and explore one barrel of oil (i.e. the cost of goods).

It is better to shut down many of the oil fields such as ocean fields and oil sands at today's $30 range. OPEC cannot cut due to the payments on the loans of many on-going ventures but they should in the future.

To supply the oil with the depressed prices would be the same as spending all the money without caring about retirement.

Summary

It is a supply and demand play. It could also be a case of commodity dumping and the U.S. may try to protect its own energy industry – you may have heard it here first.

The Losers: OPEC. They tried to cut the price to bankrupt the shale energy ventures. You do not want to shake a baby too hard or drop a big stone on your own toe. Many will lose their jobs in energy fields and the railroad industry due to shipping less coal.

The Winners: Investors who buy at low prices now and wait patiently for the long term. I hope we're in this role. As history has shown, the crisis most likely will be a profit potential.

Oil and the market

Today the consumers benefit from low gas prices. Airlines benefit too if they have not hedged on fuels or are not forced to buy at fixed prices from foreign countries. However, the stocks tank with the fall of the oil prices, so the savings in driving for most of us is not worth it.

Some still argue that oil prices will go to $10. If it does, I will keep on buying. As from today's $28 to $10, you lose about $18 or about 65%. However, it has the potential to go back to $120 and that would be more than 400% return from $28 and 1,200% return from $10. I'm buying OIL, an ETN (similar to ETF) that is supposed to float with oil price. UWTI (3X leverage) can triple your money in either direction. I do not recommend UWTI as in one day it could wipe out your entire investment. Ignore the weekly fluctuations due to speculation by traders and look for the long term.

Usually falling oil price would benefit the market in general. However, falling too much as of today is not good for the economy. Usually the market is opposite of the oil price. Today it is an exception due to the oil producing countries including the Saudis and Russia dumping foreign equities to meet their obligations. I predicted that when the oil price is at $85 per barrel, then there will be less dumping of foreign equities and the high oil will affect the market (or the market will be in the opposite direction from the oil price again). The world economies are interconnected today better than before. When the U.S. market suffers, most other global markets suffer too. In addition, when there are major withdrawals from the U.S. funds, the fund managers have to sell their foreign holdings.

China cannot build storage fast enough. They need the oil as they're blessed with polluting coal but not with oil (even oil does not generate a lot of electricity). I recommend that China buys the futures of n years at y price. This will resolve the current fluctuations and bring back the market which would not correlate with the oil price. Some argued that oil prices have reached its peak and its average price is $35 for the last 70 years. He did not consider inflation. It is a big deal for 70 years – I remember I paid $1 for a Big Mac dinner 35 years ago and today it is about $7. He also did not consider all the easy oil has left – the oil that can be extracted without much drilling. Today the production cost for off-shore drilling or from oil sand is more than $35 per barrel. There are many articles on this topic on oil. Just google "Oil Price". Here is one: 1.

Update as of 5/2016: Barron's prediction is mostly wrong as oil has passed $45 per barrel. It is due to unexpected events such as the fire in Canada.

I bought OIL in Jan. 19, 2016 (one of my purchases in this period). I expected it to increase in price by 50% as the oil does, but it only increased 25%. What happened to half of my profit? Consider USO as an alternative to OIL.

Expecting the oil price to appreciate, it is better to bet on oil service companies instead of OIL. Here is an article on how to play the oil commodity and a site on energy ETFs. I have the annualized returns of energy ETFs and CVX from Jan. 19, 2016 to May, 12, 2016.

Symbol	Description	Ann. Return
OIL	Crude oil	33%
USO	US Oil Fund ETF	112%
OIH	Oil services	80%
XOP	SPDR Oil & Gas	138%
IYE	iShr DJ US Energy	75%
XLE	S&P Energy	76%
CVX	Chevron	81%
Average		85%
SPY		32%

Exploring uranium

China will have 25 or so nuclear generators on-line by 2020, 4 years away from this writing. I hope it would give this metal a boost. With Japan's problem, uranium demand was at its historical low after inflation adjustment. We need to account for the old (more than 30 years) nuclear generators that will be decommissioned. However, the net gain is still substantial.

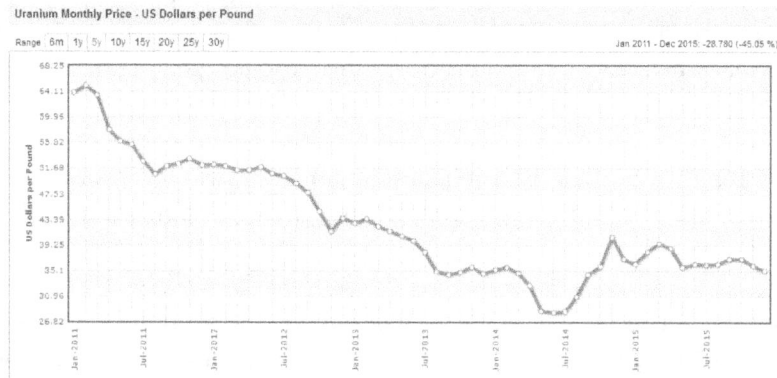

Source: Index Mundi

The price fell from 60 to 27 and rebounded to the current 35. The Monday quarterback would tell you to buy it at 27. Similar with oil, it is not unreasonable to double the price. The question is when. It could be 3 years or as high as 15 years.

Mining could be a different story as they need to survive from this depressed price. URA is the only ETF I can find with uranium and over 100 M. URA has many mining companies included. I will evaluate the companies in the future and at the current time frame, it is too risky for me.

An updated article on uranium.
https://seekingalpha.com/article/4252305-uranium-market-background-potential-investment-cameco

3   Reasons for the Coming Market Crash

This is an **example** for 2021 only. For the last few years, most market predictors have had their crystal balls broken. It is due to the excessive supply of money that leads to a non-correlation of the economy and the stock market. It cannot last forever. It will correlate again when the money supply is reduced.

The incredible recovery of the market from 2007-8 is due to the excessive printing of money (i.e. money supply). History is repeated again in 2020. It leads to easy credit to buy stock (margin debt) and buyouts/corporate profits. With more money to buy stocks and fewer stocks to buy (buyouts), it is a simple case of Supply and Demand.

Since World War II, we never had a down year in a year just before the election including 2007 and 2019. However, 2021 could be a tough year and the market bubble may finally burst. As usual, there are two camps arguing in opposite directions for predicting the market direction of 2021. I recommend my readers to take some actions, the same as buying insurance. As of 1/2021, the market is unsound fundamentally but sound technically. When the technical is unsound, it is the time to leave the market as indicated by the simple market timing illustrated in this book.

Consult your financial advisor before taking any actions, and I am not responsible for your gains or losses.

Good News

- We have hopes on the ending of this pandemic at least reducing the impact in 2021.
- The economy is improving slowly except in some sectors that are affected immensely by the pandemic.
- Energy cost could be bottom that is good for the energy sector. Judging by the forward P/Es of many energy companies, I do not believe green energy would take over in 2021.

- The interest rate is almost zero that is good for the housing sector and related sectors, buybacks, margin interest rate and investing by the corporations.

Bad News

- It has been one of the longest bull market.
- The economy is poor compared to one year ago with high unemployment rate.
- Many small businesses such as restaurants will be closed for ever.
- The record-high market is a bubble to many.
- Margin debt is in the record high.
- The government is running out of tools to revive the economy such as lowering interest rate. Excessive supplying of money will hurt the economy in the longer term.
- The national debts (partly due to our endless wars) and obligations (partly due to our aging population) are high as a percentage of the GDP.
- Most foreign countries except Japan have been reducing buying our national debt. Most of the debts were purchased by the Fed by printing money excessively.
- Many retailers that cannot service their debts will bankrupt if not already.
- The USD is weak and the status of a reserve currency is shaken. However, a weak USD is good for export, but not good for the profit for global companies.
- I expect higher inflation is coming.

Summary

2021 could be very risky. We're living dangerously on borrowed time. Hence, be conservative. The recent rise of the market is due to supply (excessive printing of money) and the demand (fixed number of assets). The market is not rational compared to the economy.

4   Winners / losers in a trade war with China

The following are based on my predictions on a full-fledged trade war with China. Buy the winners and short the losers. When the trade war is settled, reverse the directions. Losers are:

- American farmers and their suppliers such as fertilizers and farm equipment will be the chief losers. The government subsidies cannot last forever. Many have already lost their farms while their products have filled up storage spaces. Currently Brazil and Argentina are filling in the gaps to supply these products to China.

- Many chip suppliers to China will lose a lot of sales as China is the chief importer. It will take at least a year for countries to take up the slack. In 10 or so years, China will develop their own chip products. Hence, they will be back to normal in 2 years, and they will face China's competition in 10 or so years.

- Many U.S. companies are still profiting in China. These days are numbered.

- China in the future will reduce their number of buying new planes from Boeing and/or switch the orders to Airbus. Today China still needs a lot of new planes and hence the effect may not be immediate. China has the largest market for airplanes.

- Australia siding with the U.S. will be a serious loser. Australia supplies China with iron ores and agriculture products.

- Many Chinese companies especially Huawei will suffer a lot even with the help from the Chinese government. Huawei could lose their popular mobile phone sales outside China when Goggle stops suppling the apps to them.

- The markets in both the U.S. and China will fail. It could lead to a global recession.

- China would withdraw Treasury that could shake our reserve currency status of our USD.

- China would limit their export of rare earth elements to us.

Winners are:

- Vietnam is the obvious the largest beneficiary from this trade war. Many factories have moved from China to Vietnam. Many are owned by Chinese. China has helped Vietnam to improve their infrastructure. It has already gained about 8% of its GDP from the new business and is experiencing an influx of direct foreign investments.

- India could be a beneficiary too. They have a lot of problems to be fixed internally. They should copy the model of China by opening a special economic zone.

- Malaysia is a winner too. China will cut the rare earth elements to the U.S. Many countries including U.S. and Australia produce these elements but they do not refine them from the ores due to the damage to the environment. Most will be refined in Malaysia instead of in China.
- Countries may replace the U.S. as the chip and product suppliers to China. Taiwan and many EU countries are obvious beneficiaries. Many of them do not want to do business with China at the fear of being punished by the U.S.
- Russia will replace the U.S. as the supplier of energy such as LNG to China. They will have a closer tie than their history has shown.
- The South East Asia countries and some South American countries such as Brazil and Argentina will benefit and replace American agricultural products for China.
- Ericsson and Nokia will be the primary supplier of a 5G network to countries that ban Huawei's products. However, Ericsson's initial implementation is very poor compared to Huawei's.
- Many companies such as Samsung and Apple will capture Huawei's mobile phone market in Europe.
- More tourists and Chinese students will come to Europe particularly the EU countries.

Some of the symbols of the affected companies and country ETF are: VNM, INDA, EWT, ARGT, ERIC and NOK.

5   Trading by headlines

On 6/29/2019, Trump and Xi seemed to settle trade war in the G20. The market would likely rise on the coming Monday. Luckily I had closed a short position. Many chip stocks would rise as they can sell their products to Huawei. I have several of these stocks expecting the trade war would be settled. The farmers and their supporting industry would breathe easier.

I bet the shipping companies would be more profitable from the news. Without doing further research, I checked out this shipping sector and found the following stocks had been up more than 4%: DHT, NM, SBLK, STNG, TNK and ASC. It was during the weekend, so your trade account should be able to trade after hours and you need to act right after the news.

I exchanged comments with Andrew McElroy, a sector rotation expert. He does not have the rules set up as in this book but he makes great trades by 'seeing' the market and using technical analysis. The following is from his article.

"The idea is fairly simple. There is more potential for profit (and loss) in individual sectors, especially when the index is trading sideways. I try to buy strong sectors which have pulled back onto support and avoid overbought sectors at resistance. I also use Elliott Wave to identify cycles of buying and selling and stages in trends."

I would like to include headlines such as Trump's election, interest rates hikes and new regulations.

When it rains in Brazil, buy coffee futures

Recently it rained too much in SE Asia, so buy rice futures. I did not trade futures, so I missed out on the opportunity and unfortunately there is no equivalent ETF for rice. In the beginning of 2012, we should know the farming crops especially corn will not be good due to the flooding and drought in different parts of the world. Act accordingly for the profit potentials.

When a war is starting in the Middle East, most likely the oil price will rise. Buy the oil ETF and sell it when the chance of the war is reduced. Many tiny drops of profit could turn into a river of profit.

Trading by headlines is profitable, but it is hard to master and is very time-consuming. Test this strategy on paper for years before you commit real money as in most strategies. Most couch potatoes read the newspaper and watch TV all day long without making a penny. He could be couch potato millionaire if he read this article, paper traded/refined the strategy and acted on it!

However, the media tend to exaggerate headlines in order to sell their ads. Ignore all the recommendations on stocks. Most likely they are outdated information and some may be used to manipulate others. Do your own research as your mother taught you that there is no free lunch.

Rules of the game

1. Do not be too emotional; ignore your past wins and losses except when using them as lessons if they are valid (i.e. educated guesses).

2. Do not trade the entire farm. Consider option, ETFs and/or small trade on stocks, which have too many other factors to be considered.

3. Trade it fast – today's headlines will not be headlines tomorrow. There are very few exceptions.

4. Where there is a winner, there is always a loser. For example, Apple was a winner with the iPhone and BlackBerry was a loser. Same for Best Buy and Circuit City.

5. Ensure you can trade after hours from your broker.

6. Do not forget when to exit for either a small profit or a small loss.

7. Quick evaluation. The headline will be gone if you do not act fast. Skip companies with poor metrics such as high debt and low earnings yield. Prefer to buy an ETF related to the headline.

8. Most likely someone has used the information before you get it. However, some info can be deducted before it occurs. Insider purchases is a good guide.

9. I recommended crude oil at $30 per barrel in Jan. 15, 2016 as the price was at rock bottom. For value sectors, you may have to wait for a long time for the market to realize its value.

10. Sometimes you ignore stock evaluations as the headline news is more important. Learn my 5-minute evaluation process of a stock (a quick way but not recommended if you have time to do thorough research):
    - From Finviz.com, enter the stock or ETF symbol. Look at how many greens in metrics over reds.
    - Check out Forward P/E (E>0 and P/E < 20), Debut / Equity (< 50%) and P/FCF (not in red color).
    - SMA20 (or SMA50 for longer holding period). If SMA20 is > 10%, it is trending up.
    - Scroll down for Insider Trade. It usually is a good buy if insiders are buying recently and heavily with market prices.
    - Be cautious on foreign and low-volume stocks.
    - If most of the above are positive, it is likely a buy. As in life, nothing is 100% certain.

If you have a hard time following the above, most likely this strategy is not for you and it is better to return to your couch. No offense.

Volatile market and headlines

As of 7/2012 (2015 too and historically a positive market in a year right before the election), the market went sideways and was influenced by headlines. 2013 had been volatile with dips and surges influenced by daily news. The trend was up though. The Federal debt problem, EU crisis... had not been resolved. Every time we had good news, the market rose, and vice versa. In this market, buy on dips (3% down from last temporary peak) and sell on temporary surges (3% up from last temporary bottom). Some use 5% instead of 3% depending on one's risk tolerance.

Trend and calendar timing

Usually following the trend is better than ignoring it.

- Many retail investors want to get rid of the losers for year-end tax planning. Buy them at year-end and sell them early next year. In the year end of 2012, it acted the opposite as folks were selling their winners expecting a larger tax bite next year but that turned out to be false.

  This could be the reason for a sell-off of Apple in year-end of 2012 and it gave us a good entry point. To me, Apple's fundamentals were sound though the media said otherwise. In a few months, Apple became a value stock from a growth stock according to the press.

- Investors are not rational and follow the market blindly. The strategy 'Buy low and sell high' works.

- We have so much good news and bad news in the same year. Ensure the bad news will not extend to worse news. Timing is everything. Buy on bad news and sell on good news; it does not work when the market plunges.

- The media influences the market. Analyze their arguments. If they exaggerate them, do the opposite.

- Over-reaction to earnings missed or gained. When the company missed the earnings by 5%, there is a very good chance the stock will be down in a year, and vice versa. However, when it missed by 1% and the stock lost by 10%, it could be a buying opportunity, particularly when it was a temporary condition and the company is fundamentally sound.

- Buy the stock at dip when a solvable problem surfaces. Sell after the problem has been resolved. Ceiling debt is such a solvable problem and it is caused by politics. In the beginning of 2013, I mentioned that the debt problem had not been resolved and we would have this ceiling debt problem periodically until it will be eventually resolved.

Scheduled events
Some events are scheduled such as earnings announcements, unemployment reports, etc. Most likely educated guesses of the outcomes have already been circulated in the web.

The last five events on the Federal debt handling (using fancy names such as sequester and debt ceiling) were scheduled such as the government shutdown. They drove the market down by about an average of 5% each time. Sell before the event and buy back afterward. The Congress has cancelled these debt deadlines as of 1/2014.

Many sectors are impacted by events such as Trump's success in election, hikes of interest rates and trade wars.

Follow the institutional investors
They drive the market. When they see the sector is over-valued or the peak has been reached, they rotate sectors.

Use deduction
In 2014, China has a great harvest on wheat, corn and rice. China's population is #1 in the world and its middle class is growing. The farmers in the US will be hurt as they cannot export these products to their number one customer. Use the same logic to deduct that there will be problems in the companies that supply products and services to the farmers. They are combines, fertilizer companies and seed companies. It further translates into Deere, Potash, Monsanto and AGCO.

Due to increasing wealth in 2017, Chinese demanded more meat. It takes a lot of corn to produce one pound of meat and in turn corn needed fertilizers. Hence, you can expect the companies producing fertilizers will increase their profits.

Geopolitical crisis
Many times no action is the best action. It applies here. I had my experience in selling too many stocks via stops in 911. The market returned in a few days and I did not buy them back.

An analysis from Ned David Research covers 51 events from 1900 to 2014. My interpretation for actions: Trade the affected sector (via sector ETF) in the first few days and reverse the trade 2 months after. Many times it means the oil price and gold price would rise.

I bought SH (a contra ETF to SPY) in August, 2017 as August and September are statistically the worst months in addition to the high risk in the current market. It is expected to be sold on Nov. 1. The North Korea crisis did not do much to the market on the first day but the market (the S&P 500) lost 1.45% and the risky NASDAQ lost 2.13% (see my blog on FAANG) on the second day.

Caveat. Need to understand the crisis. If it would lead to World War 3, most sectors will not recover for a long while. Again, there is no sure thing in investing otherwise there would be no poor folks. However, educated guesses should materialize more often than not.

My experiences
- When the interest rates is expected to rise, plan on investments that are favorable to it and vice versa.
- On the same week, CROX lost almost 40% in one day. I bought some and made about 10% profit in a week. CROX's fundamentals were no good and it did have a history of a roller coaster ride in its stock price. After a year, I found out that I sold it too early as the stock price doubled. Better to buy a stock on its way up than down unless we identify that the bottom has been reached.
- I was on vacation while the second incident of the Boeing Max happened. Should have shorted the stock. In addition, Boeing's suppliers would suffer too similar to Apple's suppliers on Apple.

  https://www.barrons.com/articles/boeing-737-max-jet-production-cut-suppliers-stocks-51554499957?siteid=yhoof2&yptr=yahoo

- I missed applying the same trick to the rise of Apple when Apple announced its new iPod. I should at least buy the stocks of its part suppliers. I hope learn from this lesson and take advantage of future similar circumstances.

I missed the opportunity to buy uranium stocks. It should be bought after Japan's disaster. When Japan approved the reopening of nuclear reactors today, these stocks including CCJ, DNN, LEU, URRE, UEC, URZ, URG and UUUU surge. When China's new nuclear reactors are on-line, they will surge again.

- Experiences in early 2014.
  Recently and in a short time, I made a good profit on BBY and a tiny profit on TGT. Both were bought due to headlines.

6   Earnings season overreactions

AAII has some screens for stocks with pleasant earnings surprises and bad earnings surprises (Jan., April, July and Oct.). The pleasant surprise screen always beats the other screens from the last time I checked.

Zacks ranks stocks with positive earnings revisions. Their stocks have ranked #1 has an amazing average annual return of 26% according to them. In 2019, the performance of recent tests did not hold up that well.

As with all vendors, we should check their recent performance (say, the last 5 years). If the strategy is proven to be effective, more investors will follow and usually make it less effective.

It usually starts on the first two weeks after the ending of quarters (Dec., March, June and September) as indicated in the following link.
http://www.investopedia.com/ask/answers/08/earnings-season.asp

My experience

Contrary to the conventional wisdom, I enjoy the negative surprises more. If the company has a reason to come back or its problem is only temporary, I buy the stock. Sometimes it takes a few months and sometimes even a year for the stock to come back. The strategy of 'Buying low and selling high' works more often than it does not. However, avoid the stocks that start their long-term plunge.

Missing expected earnings by 1% and causing the stock to drop by 10% is a buy to me. Heading to bankruptcy is a different story though.

My momentum strategy buys stocks with positive earnings revisions. I usually do not keep these stocks for over a month.

As of today (4/6/2016), the quarter earnings season is starting. This year I have worry about the earnings due to the strong USD. It would impact the earnings as about 40% (my rough estimate) of the incomes of global companies are from foreign countries. If we feel there will be more disappointments, we should short the stocks that are expected to have poor earnings.

My lesson

Take advantage of the irrational human reactions. Retail investors and institutional investors are both human beings. Fund managers have more pressure to sell a loser to keep their jobs. Retail investors usually sell after the big institutional investors. Try to find out whether it is just a sentimental reaction or the stock is going to fall further.

How to hedge your stocks from earning surprises

Stocks might have a wide swing after the earnings announcements. Hedge the unfavorable announcements by the following three methods:

1. Stop loss.
    Usually the swing is steeper than your stop price. When the price reaches or go below a specific price, it will be turned into a market sell order. Institutional investors usually unload the stocks faster than the retail investors, opposite of buying. However, their positions are huge. We can tell they are unloading (or loading) from the unusual high trading volumes of the stocks. Ensure that your trades are allowed after hours.

2. Option.

It is like buying an insurance to protect your loss. Protect yourself from large losses as insurance is not cheap and smaller losses could be due to volatility.

3. Earnings prediction.
    They are also known as whispers or educated guesses. Zacks has a grading system.

    Also insiders know the earnings before their announcements. However, it is illegal to use this information before its announcement.

Earnings revisions will be available before the announcement and they would provide better guesses to the announcement. With today's dividend chasers, the announcement of dividends or its increase would boost the stock price.

Personally I do not do a lot to protect my stocks from earnings announcements. I have too many stocks. However, when we have evaluated the stocks correctly and monitor them regularly, we should have more pleasant surprises.

Profit from earnings surprises
The stock price usually rises on positive earnings surprises and falls otherwise. Sometimes they are not rational such as 1% miss in earnings that causes 10% loss in the stock price. In some rare cases, the positive earnings causes the stock to plunge as the investors expected better earnings even better than consensus. Here is the example of looking for finding stocks with positive earnings (you can profit by buying puts or shorting the stocks for stocks with negative earnings).

- Find stocks that have earnings announcements next week or month. Sources are Finviz.com's screener and SeekingAlpha.
- The screened stocks should fit some basic criteria. My criteria are: Market Cap > 200M, stock price > $2, average volume > 10,000 shares...
- If you subscribe to Zacks, check out the earnings grade. Stocks with Grade 1 and Grade 2 deserve our time for further research.

- If there are meaningful insiders' purchases, the chance of positive earnings are high.
- A positive short-term trend (SMA-20% from Finviz.com) is a plus.
- A positive short-term trend for the sector that stock belongs to is a plus. The sector can be represented by an ETF for that sector and use SMA-20%.
- Read articles on the stock for a qualitative analysis. Find these articles from many sources including SeekingAlpha. Today they have fewer articles for free.

Be warned that we do not expect all wins. When we achieve more than 50% wins, we should fare very well financially. When the market is falling or the earnings are expected to be poor, do not buy stocks except those that are fundamentally sound.

Take advantage of others' orders

1. Ensure your account can trade after hours.
2. Use Finviz.com to look for stocks announcing earnings this week. Prefer fundamentally sound stocks with a market cap great than 500 (100 for smaller stocks).
3. Check out earningswhispers.com. They have two estimates: the consensus and the one from this website. Write down the exact time too.
4. If you subscribe Zacks.com, use its rating too as a reference.
5. Be at least 15 minutes earlier than the announcement date and time.
6. Google the stock and EPS from Google News. Refresh the search every 2 minutes. Check related articles.
7. If it beats the estimates, buy it at least one penny less than the last trade price and sell it within a day or two. The logic is to take advantage of all those orders that have not considered earnings in a timely fashion. It does not always work.
8. To improve performance, include Revenue with EPS.

Personally I do not do it as it is too time-consuming for me; my beauty sleep is more important than money. Again test it out before committing real money. There are many parameters that can be tuned to adjust to your personal preferences and the current market conditions. This is the essence of an entire book. I read with my own enhancements such as using Finviz.com.

*** Bonus: Technical Analysis (TA)

Technical analysis (TA) is the analysis of the price movements and the short-term trend and possible reversal, while fundamental analysis focuses on metrics such as price/earnings ratio and debts. TA assumes the future stock price behavior can be determined by the patterns of past price behavior – it is true more times than untrue. Traders use TA a lot and can profit by shorting stocks. Investors can use them to find the entry points and exit points and some investors only buy stocks with a positive long-term trend (using SMA-200%).

Many times stock analysis based on fundamentals fails when the evaluation is solely based on fundamentals. Technical Analysis (TA) has the following characteristics:

- Most of the time, TA is profitable in the short term (less than 3 months). The weather man is more accurate in tomorrow's weather rather than a month away. TA can also signal the reversals.
- There are too many signals if you have more than three TA parameters. To start, use SMA (Simple Moving Average) and RSI(14); both are available in Finviz.com without charting.
- You can combine TA with fundamentals such as a rising SMA50 with increasing Insider Purchases. In addition, you can use more than one TA indicator.
- For market timing, TA is a huge part, but many fundamentals should be considered too. You can use similar techniques to time the market and time stocks and/or sectors such as Golden Cross / Death Cross.

Technical analysis wins for the following reasons:
- Information such as a new product or a major lawsuit pending is not reflected timely in fundamentals, but rather in technical analysis. It gives us guidance in understanding the trend of a stock or even the entire market.
- Most TAs are based on accumulated data. For example, if RSI(14) is greater than 65, most likely this stock is overbought. If there is no reason for this condition, you may consider selling it.

- When too many investors follow TA, it would become self-prophecy.
- Do not act against the trend. The fundamentalist may buy a stock when it loses 50%, the TA investor most likely will not buy it. Many times the losing stocks will lose another 25% or so. The TA investor most likely buys it on the way up only or short it on the way down.

An example. NVRO (a stock symbol) has appreciated about 100% from mid Feb. to Oct. in 2016 despite its poor fundamentals. It has a new product that could revolutionize physical healing and eliminate pain that will not be shown in the fundamentals except by the eventual Forward P/E. Technical charts can inform us of the uptrend.

Volume is the confirmation. Institution investors drive the market. When the market (esp. the S&P 500 stocks) is down and the volume is up, there is good chance institution investors are dumping their holdings. It is obvious when most of the indicators are promising but the volume is small.

Info from free websites.
Use "Head and shoulder" as an example. Obtain the description by typing "Head and shoulder" in Investopedia. Obtain more info by entering same in the search under YouTube.

Links:
Before you trade:
https://www.youtube.com/watch?v=8hM18AHcUCs
A strategy: https://www.youtube.com/watch?v=asDBegQaupM

1   Technical analysis (TA)

The basics
Technical analysis (a.k.a. charting) is easier to learn than you might expect. It represents the trend of the market (a stock or a group of stocks) graphically. If more investors are in the market, the market would move upwards until it changes direction. We divide the trends into short-term, intermediate-term and long-term.

The chartists usually do not consider fundamentals as they believe they have already been priced into the stock price and some fundamentals are not available to the public. To illustrate, a new drug has been discovered, the stock price of the company jumps initially by insiders purchases and the informed. Its fundamental metrics do not demonstrate this right away, but many investors are buying to boost up the stock price as evidenced by the technical indicators such as SMA for 20 or 50 days.

The volume is a confirmation. When the stock moves up or down by 10% with a low volume, the trend is not yet confirmed.

The trend of the stock price is not a straight line in most cases. Hence a trend line is usually drawn to indicate the direction of the stock. Many investors believe the stocks fluctuate in certain ranges (i.e., channels) and the chart draws the upper value (the resistance line) and the lower value (the support line). In theory, the price of a stock fluctuates within the resistance line (ceiling for understanding) and support (floor). When it reaches its support, it becomes a buy and vice versa for a sell. Most charts including Finviz.com would display these lines.

When the price passes out of the channel, it is called a breakout. Darvas, one of the oldest and most successful chartists, profited from the breakouts of the resistance line and believed the stock was close to the support line of the new channel. Hence it would be a long way up in theory.

If it were so simple, there will be no poor folks
It works most of the time, but do not place all your money on it. For chartists, 51% is great (the same for playing Black Jack). Some trends reverse very fast such as the bio drug stocks in 2015. You need to hedge your bets such as placing stop orders. Most do not want to spend their lives watching the trend from a big screen.

Most novices use too many technical indicators and lose in their performances to the professionals. Recently, most chartists were not doing all that great and I did not find many books on their success than a decade ago. It could be due to too many followers in similar setups. I verified it with my recent testing using Finviz.com.

Simple Moving Average

The basic technical indicator is SMA-N. It is the average of the last N trade sessions. To illustrate, if N is 15 and the exchange is open during this period, you need 3 weeks (21 days) of data. When N is 20 (or SMA-20), we classify it as short-term. Similarly, SMA-50 is an intermediate-term and SMA-200 is long-term. I prefer 50, 100 and 250. This trend duration is important. For example, do not want to place long-term purchases using the short-term SMA-50. There are many modifications to SMA such as giving more weight to recent data, but I have not found them any better. Finviz.com includes this information without charting (SMA-20, SMA-50 and SMA-100 in percentages).

Defining the trend periods is rather arbitrary. I use SMA-350 to detect the market plunges and SMA-100 for stocks. Weighted Moving Average weighs more weight on recent price data.

It can be used to determine whether we are in a bull, a bear or a sideways market using SMA-50 (or SMA-200 for longer term) for the market (using SPY), the sector (using an ETF for the sector and the specific stock. The trend is up when the price is above the SMA and the reversal of the trend.
https://www.youtube.com/watch?v=jdYNaE5GJ0k

The trend is your best friend

Most traders use TA for trending in a short duration. Investors can also use TA to time the entry and exit points for better potential profits. Value investors usually are patient and they do bottom fishing and they search for 'oversold' conditions using RSI(14). Again, high volume is a confirmation.

Many sites provide charting free of charge such as Yahoo!Finance. Finviz.com provides a lot of technical indicators without charting such as SMA% and RSI(14). It also provides screen searching for stocks that meet your technical analysis criteria.

Hands on

Bring up Finviz.com and enter any stock symbol such as AAPL. You can see the daily prices of AAPL from about nine months ago to today. Three SMAs (Simple Moving Average) are displayed as SMA-20, SMA-50 and SMA-200. The first two are for short-term trends.

When the price is above the SMA, it is expected to be trending up. Again, the trade volume is used as a confirmation.

You can also see the resistance line and the support line drawn. In theory, the stock will trade within these lines. When it exceeds its resistance line, it is called a breakout, and vice versa for a breakdown. Sometimes it displays some technical patterns such as Cup and Shoulder and Double Down (both are positive patterns).

Select Weekly data. The Candle chart is better described than the Daily chart. Candles give us better descriptions of the price: open, close, high and low. The green color indicates the price is up for the period (a week in this example) and the red color indicates a down period.

In addition, Finviz.com includes some technical indicators in the metric section such as RSI. Most other chart sites are similar in the basics. Use Finviz's Help and select Technical Analysis for more description. Investopedia has enhanced descriptions on this topic.

TA patterns
There are many TA patterns such as Bollinger Bands and MACD. The patterns are based on the stock prices and many times they prove to be correct predictions especially on stocks with high volume and high market caps. Patterns have been repeating themselves many times as they are driven by investors.

Sites for TA
There are many free sites for charts with explanations of their technical indicators. Popular ones include BigCharts.com, SmallCharts.com and Yahoo!Finance. Fidelity includes some unique features in its charts such as P/E.

Why I do not use TA as a primary tool for stock picking
My investing style is different from a day trader. I prefer to 'Buy Low and Sell High' instead of 'Buy High and Sell Higher'. I try to find the real bottom price. TA will not find the bottom very easily but it tracks the trend better. As a bargain hunter, I do not expect the stock will rise fast as I'm usually swimming against the tide. However, value stocks could stay in the low price for a long time

(i.e., value trap). I like to select stocks that turn around as evidenced by the SMA-20 and SMA-50.

With that said, my momentum portfolio has appreciated consistently and usually has the best performing stocks among all my portfolios. It is based on the timely grade from my subscriptions plus the metrics on TA timing.

Most chartists would also tell you to buy the stocks that have broken out (i.e., higher than the resistance line) and/or stocks at their highs. Contrary to value investing, you should exit when the trend reverses. The reversal could happen very fast and hence protect your portfolio by setting up stop loss (preferably with trailing stop) orders.

My opinion. I do not want to argue whether TA is good for you or not. You need to find that out. Most likely, the day traders and very short-term traders will profit more from TA than the investors seeking value stocks for the long-term gains.

Random remarks
Even if you do not use technical analysis, you should spend some time learning it. It is better to marry fundamentals and TA. My random remarks are:
- The Institutional investors (insurance companies, pension funds, mutual funds, etc.) use TA and they MOVE the market. A lot of times it becomes a self-fulfilling prophecy. It is better to join them as most of us cannot beat them.
- Day traders take advantage of the institutional investors by spotting their trends and jumping on the wagon.
- Most TA stocks should be good sized and have large average daily volumes. I prefer to use TA on value stocks to prevent long-term losses.
- I do know some folks making big money using TA, but I know more making good money using fundamentals. Since TA predicts the market better in the shorter term, its practitioners may have to pay higher taxes (in today's tax laws) in taxable accounts.
- Our objective should be making money with the least risk. Once you claim to belong to a certain group of either

Fundamental or TA, you will be biased and forget your primary objective in investing.

- TA tracks the last two big market plunges (2000 and 2007) pretty well. The chart will not warn you right away for the upcoming plunge (as it depends on past data) to avoid the initial losses, but they will warn you to avoid bigger losses.
- You can use TA to short the stock, the sector, the country or the market.
- Risk management (with stops to reduce losses and trailing stops for rising stocks) and trade positions (more positions on stocks with better potential) could make you a fortune, even if you have only 50% correct.
- Your desire, passion, discipline, knowledge and hand-on skill (including learning from your successes and failures) are the keys to success. A well-tested strategy and TA tools to time the trend of a stock, sector and the market are the tools.

Afterthoughts
Besides searching for stocks that have potential breakouts, we should check the stocks we own for potential breakdowns.
Technical Analysis tutorial.
https://www.YouTube.com/watch?v=GENBVwV8PMs

SMA tutorial.
https://www.YouTube.com/watch?v=Na-ctpPsnks

Links
Fidelity video: Technical Analysis
https://www.fidelity.com/learning-center/technical-analysis/chart-types-video

Filler: The 0.5%
The world has been controlled by 0.5% who are the wealthiest and make the rules of the world. These folks own US businesses and EU businesses, and they make money in every way and everywhere they see opportunities. The following link and Tesla's mega factory in China forced me to think; it is a case of Biden vs the 0.5%.
https://finance.yahoo.com/news/citigroup-hire-1-700-people-093000440.html

2   Examples of using TA

I have outlined how we can spot market plunges using TA and I use it to monitor the market every three months or so (I recommend doing it every month and even more frequently when the market is risky). Here is an example of how to use it to trade individual stocks.

I have to admit I do not use TA that much on individual stocks and clearly I am not an expert in TA. If this article stirs up your interest, read more books or attend seminars / classes on TA. However, this book describes the basic and most useful technical indicators. There are many good and free articles from Investopedia on this topic. Personally, I prefer to seek fundamentally sound companies at bargain prices and wait for their full appreciation. It has been proven to me many times over.

TA is very useful for momentum and day traders. With the rising volume, you can detect that the stocks are traded by managers of mutual funds, hedge funds, insurance companies and pension funds, and you profit by riding on their wagons.

Some stocks are good for TA. Usually, they are larger companies with above-average volumes and are fundamentally sound. Avoid the stocks that are trending downwards unless you're bottom fishing. Let me pick CSCO (a cyclical stock) for an illustration. I bought it several times in 2012. I sold some in 2013 and 2014 making good profits. This is quite different from what short-term traders would use during the following:

The green line is a 50-day simple moving average (SMA) for the following chart using one year data.

Buy the stock when it is above its SMA and sell when it is below. Following the chart would make good money based on this simple rule. Also, practice the strategy "Sell on May 1, Buy back on Nov. 1".

Not all stocks follow this profitable pattern. Fundamentalists may try to pick the bottom in late July while chartists enter positions on its upward trend. The chartists have an advantage to stay away from stocks in their downward trend.

Exponential Moving Average has better predictable power as it weighs more on recent prices. Some indicators / patterns work better in specific market conditions – all markets are different.

Volume is important as a confirmation. If the price of a stock is up with thin volume, the rise is questionable and it could be manipulated.

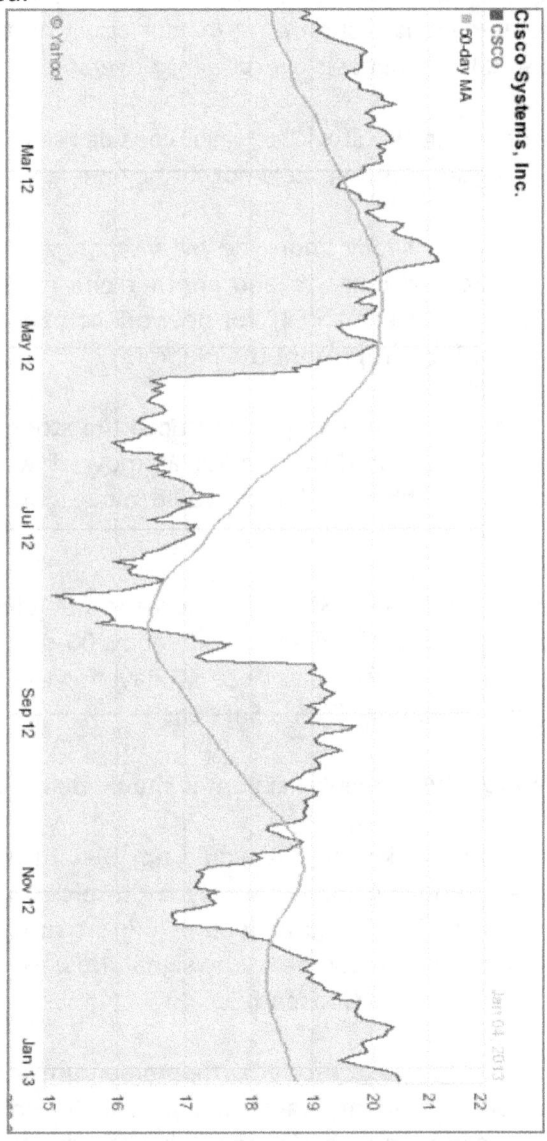

Table: CSCO   50-day SMA   Source: Yahoo!Finance

(https://ebmyth.blogspot.com/2020/09/table-csco-50-day-sma.html)

We can improve the trades by:

- Use a different moving average in the number of days (50 in this example) and other indicators such as EMA (a moving average that weighs higher on more recent data). It may improve prediction accuracy and/or cut down on the number of trades. RSI(14) suggests overbought / oversold conditions.

- Instead of selling the stock for cash, consider selling the stock short. Selling short is definitely not for beginners.

- The accuracy is usually improved by a separate chart for the sector the stock belongs to and another one for the market. For CSCO, you can use an ETF for network companies and SPY (or a similar ETF) to represent the market.

  In theory and in theory only, when both the stock, the sector that the stock is in and the market all move down, the stock price has a high chance that it would move down, and vice versa.

  We use the 50 days (in SMA) for short-term holding of stocks (20 for even shorter holding periods and 200 days for longer holding periods). Personally, I use 30 days for the sector ETF. Again, 'Days' is actually 'Trade Sessions'.

TA is not for most fundamentalists but it should be used

For a bargain hunter like me, TA would not benefit me a lot for picking stocks at their bottoms. I would try to pick up CSCO with prices ranging from 15-17 and all well below the moving average line, but TA would not show me a Buy signal. However, for short-term swing traders TA is a Godsend.

To me, TA is a good indicator for growth, momentum and for short-term trading. Some fundamentalists may use TA for entry and exit points. Some recommend buying the stock when the price is above the SMA-200 (same as when SMA-200% is positive and that can be readily obtained from Finviz.com).

It should be profitable for using the 'Buy High and Sell Higher' strategy, provided you protect your profits effectively. This is also called 'Buy at a reasonable cost'. One's opinion.

In selecting a tool, you have to understand how, and why to use it and whether it fits your investing style. I use TA for market timing for the entire market more than on individual stocks. When I have more time, I probably would use TA more frequently.

Most of us cannot spot the bottom of a stock; I have had some success but most likely they were due to luck. When a stock is moving up from the bottom, there is a good chance it will move further up. TA shows it and the volume confirms it.

Conclusion
Even a fundamentalist like me can benefit a lot by using TA. This book touches on the very basics of TA.

Besides monitoring the fundamentals of the stocks you bought once every 6 months, you should analyze their technical indicators more often (1 month to 3 months depending on your available time). When the market is risky (close to the SMA average), run the SMA chart more frequently (say once a week).

Rule-based   trading:
https://www.youtube.com/watch?v=GAH9EyydEsM

---

3   Easy TA without charts

Bring up Finviz.com from your browser. Enter the stock you're evaluating. SMA-200% stands for Simple Moving Average of the last 200 trade sessions. RSI(14)% is the relative strength index for the last 14 trade sessions.

The following is just a suggestion with conservative parameters. Adjust the parameters according to your risk tolerance and requirements. Do not buy the stock with SMA-200% is < 0 (trending down), SMA-200% > 40 (peaking), or RSI(14)% > 65 (overbought).

Link: RSI: https://www.youtube.com/watch?v=VH84ppzmq9Q

4　Bollinger Bands

Bollinger Bands have been proven useful for traders. In theory, the stock is traded between the upper band and the lower band forming an envelope. For more info, click the following link.

http://www.investopedia.com/terms/b/bollingerbands.asp
https://www.youtube.com/watch?v=wfPf-KBuQH0

The following chart was drawn by Yahoo!Finance for CSCO from 8/7/2012 to 8/7/2014 selecting Bollinger Bands for the 50 days as a parameter. If you trade more often, use 20 days. If the chart is too small to display on your screen, enter the following in your PC's browser.
http://ebmyth.blogspot.com/2014/08/screen-csco-bollinger-bands-50.html

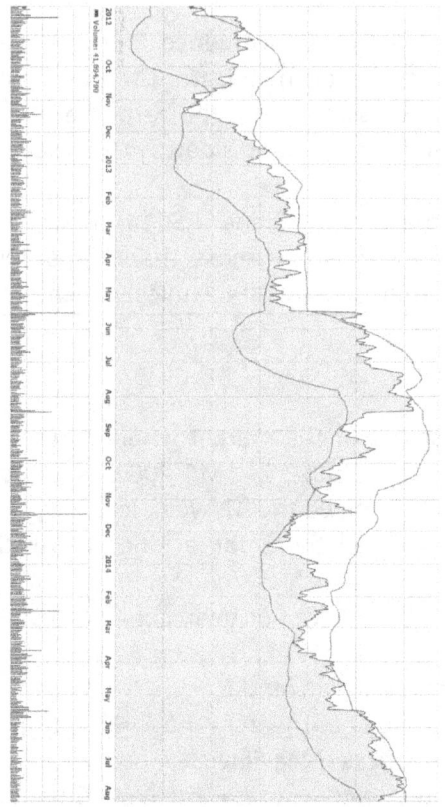

Bollinger Bands 50 Days.　Source: Yahoo!Finance

You buy the stock when the price is close to the lower band and sell the stock when it is close to the upper band.

When the stock price passes the upper band, it is called a breakout. Similar for the stock falling below the lower band. From the above, we should make some good money.

It is advisable to use at least one more technical indicator. I recommend the RSI(14), which is also accessible from Yahoo!Finance or similar sites. When it is above 70, it is overbought, so I recommend selling the stock. When it is below 30, it is oversold, so I recommend buying the stock. However, fundamentals have not been considered. Some stocks just go to zero and some just surge.

5   MACD

MACD, Moving Average Convergence Divergence, is an effective momentum (i.e., short-term) indicator used by most traders. When the stock price is crossing above the zero line, it is a buy and vice versa. It may give false signals in sideways fluctuation.
###
Again, try to master SMA and RSI(14) first. Using too many indicators usually harms you more than helps you. You can use Finviz.com to search stocks with technical indicators.

A TA strategy

Buy the stock, sector or the market when: 1. The SMA-50% (from Finviz) is above SMA-200%, 2. SMA-200% is positive, and 3. The price is at least 25% above the 52-week low (i.e., do not buy at the bottom as it may stay there for a long while). Sell, vice versa. Consider other metrics such as Volume, P/E, Debt / Equity, etc. It is great in concept, but I have not been convinced so far in my recent tests.
Related YouTube: Shorter Trend
https://www.youtube.com/watch?v=GAH9EyydEsM
Finding breakout stocks using Finviz.
https://www.youtube.com/watch?v=bWpe30R2VnM
Picking bottom: https://www.youtube.com/watch?v=ygj0TPqmRK4
A TA strategy: https://www.youtube.com/watch?v=ygj0TPqmRK4

Another strategy: CCI + MA
https://school.stockcharts.com/doku.php?id=technical_indicators:
commodity_channel_index_cci
https://www.youtube.com/watch?v=CuWzDo72-Rk

6   Other TA indicators/patterns

They are briefly mentioned here. Click on the links or use Investopedia for more descriptions.

Double Bottom is a bullish pattern as the support line is stronger than the resistance line.
Double Top is the opposite and is a bearish pattern. I prefer the price of the second top is less than the price of the first top. It seems there is no enough investment in this stock to break out of the second top.

Resistance and Support. The stock is supposed to fluctuate between an imaginary zone of resistance and support. Short-term traders may sell when the price is close to the resistance line and close any short positions when it is close to the support line. However, breakouts from this zone are possible and many traders trade stocks on breakouts. It is a little similar to 52-week highs and lows. The trend line indicates the trend of the stock.

Cup and handle is a bullish pattern. The stock price peaks and then forms a shape of a cup and handle.

Head & Shoulder is a bearish pattern while the reversed Head & Shoulder is a bullish pattern. It signals that the peak (the head) has been reached and the second top (the shoulder) has failed to reach the previous peak.

Stochastic Oscillator. It is similar to RSI(14). Many traders use this indicator. If it is above 65, it is overbought. If it is below 30, it is oversold. In general, I would trade on an uptrend when the stock is moving from 60 to 85; it depends on how volatile the stock is. It is better to use with other indicators and as a reference.

To illustrate when to buy, one suggestion is to buy when this indicator changes to an uptrend while the price is still going down.

Many traders follow these technical indicators and SMA. They could become "self-fulfilled" prophecies.

Link

Chart patterns. https://www.youtube.com/watch?v=o6hZma0bajE
More: https://www.youtube.com/watch?v=aRlWle9smww
Resistance: https://www.youtube.com/watch?v=C2qRW9_via4

7   More on technical analysis

This chapter describes some TA indicators that can help us. Click on the following links for a better description.

- Finviz.com.
  It has SMA20%, SMA50% and SMA200% to represent the short-term, intermediate-term and the long-term indicator. SMA stands for Simple Moving Average and n for days for the duration of the average (for example, 20 days for SMA20%).

  If you are a long-term investor, use SMA-200% (or SMA-350%). Using SMA-20% would cause a lot of sells / reentries, which costs more in trading fees.

  Buy when the price is above the Moving Average line and sell when the price is below it. Finviz.com provides the percent of moving above the moving average to indicate just how much the price deviates from the average.

  If you hold the stock for an average of 50 days, use SMA50%, and so on. If you hold stocks for an average of 90 days, you have to create your own SMA using one of the many websites including Yahoo!Finance and specify 90 days for the period.

Try other similar technical indicators such as EMA, which is supposed to weigh more on the more recent data. A weather man can predict tomorrow's weather better than the weather a week away.

- RSI(14) indicates whether the stock is overbought or oversold. RSI oscillates between zero and 100. Traditionally, and according to Wilder (the author of this method), RSI is considered overbought with a value above 70 and oversold with a value below 30 as described in the article.

When it is oversold, most likely the stock will fall, and vice versa.

(http://stockcharts.com/school/doku.php?id=chart_school:technical_indicators:relative_strength_index_rsi)

Click here for another article.
(http://financial-dictionary.thefreedictionary.com/Relative+Strength+Index)

- Cup and handle is a popular indicator of when the stock price would surge.
(http://www.investopedia.com/terms/c/cupandhandle.asp)

- Double bottom indicates that the stock will move up.
(http://stockcharts.com/school/doku.php?id=chart_school:chart_analysis:chart_patterns:double_bottom_revers)

It shows a double bottom for Apple in 2013.

- A trading strategy:
https://www.youtube.com/watch?v=asDBegQaupM

8 Using Fidelity

Click "Research and News" and then "Stock". Simple charting and advanced charting are both provided.

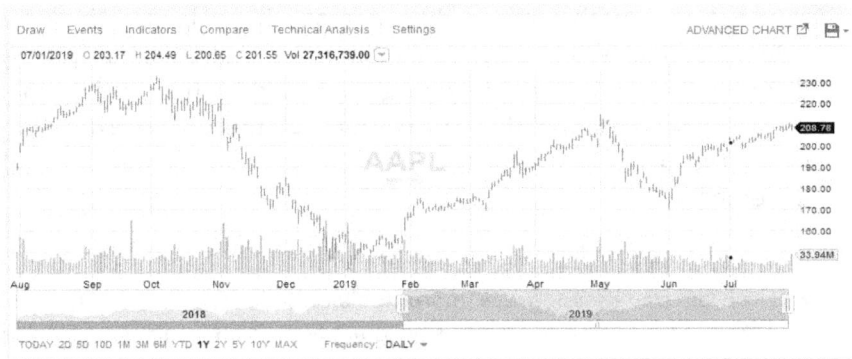

Hints:

- Fidelity provides suggested stops.
- Click on the Support and Resistance under Technical Analysis to display the Resistance Line (upper limit). Click on the Resistance Line and you can get the Support Line (lower limit).
- Click on Advanced Chart and then click on "learn how to use the chart".
- Under Advanced Chart, select Draw and Trend Line. Select the upper line by touching the highest points and do the same for the lower line.

9 Determine the exit point

I have described 2 exit strategies: Death Cross and SMA-350 (or SMA-400 for fewer false alarms). This is a bonus technique used stand alone or together with the above two. The concept is simple, but it requires more understanding on the charting and candlestick. All the three techniques can be applied to individual stocks, sectors and the market. We demonstrate it with the market using SPY, and the reentry point is just the opposite.

All the three techniques do not identify the top and the bottom as they are based on past data. However, it tells you to exit to avoid further losses. All three have false alarms, but this one could exit earlier. We can tune all the techniques to have fewer false alarms, but it would increase more losses than the original techniques.

The institutional investors (mutual funds, pension funds, etc.) move the market. That's why the volume is important. Whenever there is high volume, most likely they are trading seriously. They may want to make the market rosier than it really is by buying, but the volume is small. When they sell a lot, most likely the market will be down for a while. The following signals that the institutional investors are selling with the exception of the option expiration dates (the Friday of the third week in March, June, September and December):

- Today's trade session is unprofitable.
- The last trade session was unprofitable or had a very tiny profit.
- The trade volume is higher than the trade volume of the last trade session; candlesticks and trade volume are available from most charts.
- The trade volume is higher than the average trade volume of the last 50 trade sessions (available from most charts).
- If the above happens more often (such as 4 times in the last month), be careful. Due to the huge number of stocks the institutional investors own, they cannot sell them fast; I estimate it takes about 2 to 4 weeks to dump the stocks.
- The market falls for no reason; the only logical reason could be the institutional investors are dumping.
- Big fall before the market open and it continues for the entire trade day. It indicates many smart moneys including the retail investors are moving out of the market.
- Most likely, Death Cross and SMA-350 (or SMA-400) would signal a down market. SMA-200 would give you a signal ahead of the described two. Using SMA-50 and SMA-200:
  https://www.youtube.com/watch?v=BaZxE12cZP4&t=218s
  https://www.youtube.com/watch?v=wMxj6iB92ZA

The deterioration of the Buy/Sell could indicate the market is falling earlier.

#Fillers
"Hold" rating from analysts means "Sell as fast as you can". Very seldom, there is a "Sell".

Epilogue

After my early retirement, I have been spending most of my time in investing, running thousands of simulation and reading over one hundred books in investing. Starting from 2000, I have been doing extraordinary good. I comment in financial blogs and save the good ones in my own blog, so I can refer them later on. After several years, I have enough information to write a book.

At first, I want to write a book for one reader only: Me. My children have better things to do than investing. I do not need to keep my 'secrets' for them. That's why I publish this book. From the version before its release, it had been doing better than my expectation. It has been very rewarding, when my readers tell me how much they enjoy and benefit from this book.

It is far more financially rewarding working on my investment including finding new strategies. Writing books and articles takes time away from my investing and it actually costs me more money. However, it has been fun to write this book and to interact with my readers. Money cannot buy everything.

I've received a lot of good responses and thanks. The 2nd Edition incorporates a lot of your feedbacks and my recent updates. Some complaints are not valid though.

- The primary objective of this book is helping you make money, not improving your English skill. Based on the techniques here, I had 50% cash (should be 100% if I followed my charts) before the correction of August, 2015. A best seller asked her readers to exit the market in the 4th edition and I bet it could be as early as 2009 in the first edition.

- One book on sector rotation has many good reviews. It is only 35 pages compared to my Sector Rotation that has 265 pages. They are in the same price range. It must be reviewed by the author's friends and family members.

- As described in Introduction, charts and tables can be displayed in the full size of your reader by selecting it. I also provide links to the more important charts so you can display them on the large screen of your PC.

If you believe this book is beneficial, please comment in amazon.com (https://www.amazon.com/dp/B01D7MYE1SP).

Appendix 1 – All my books

Book	No. of Pages	Link	ebook	Rating /5
Art of investing 5th Edition	590	Click here	link	4.5
Sector Rotation: 21 strategies 5th Edition	500	Click here	Link	9.5/10
Be a stock expert in 5 minutes. Expanded Edition.	203	Click here	Link	
Using Finviz 5th Edition	600	Click here	Link	4.5
Using Fidelity 5th Edition	600	Click here	Link	4.5
Momentum Investing 3rd Edition	285	Click here	Link	
Using profitable investing sites	520	Click here	link	
Investing successes and plunders	410	Click here	Link	
Best stocks to buy for 2025	375	Click here	Link	
Profit from bull, bear and sideway market	240	See ebook	Link	4
Artificial intelligence investing	420	See ebook	Link	
Profitable covered call	615		Link	4
Your best dollar for smart investing. $1 all the time.	65		Link	4

The ratings are usually done by ChatGPT and/or DeepSeek (AI) which

the most unbiased.

If you already have my book that is over 400 pages, most likely you do not need to buy the above books except "Investing successes and plunders" and the "Best Stock" series, which may be available every December with the title such as "Best stocks for 2026" – not a promise.

For paper-bag readers, access the links via the following link. https://www.blogger.com/blog/post/edit/7608574268453692676/1786802320953936467

Full AI reviews on my books and articles: TonyP4Idea: Summary of AI reviews on my work

Most books have paperbacks. Links and offers are subject to change without notice. If most of your investing are in momentum/sector rotation, select "Sector Rotation 5th Edition". If not, select one from "Art of Investing 5th Edition", "Using Fidelity 5th Edition" and "Using Finviz 5th *Editon*"

.

*** AI Reviews:

Many thanks to the most unbiased reviews by AI. I received 4/5 stars for most of my books – it could be the highest AI would give besides the classics. Unless otherwise specified, most reviews were done in Feb., 2025. For the full review, click on the above link for the specific book.

Sector Rotation 5th Edition

Rating: 9.5/10

Sector Rotation: 5th Edition is arguably **the most complete book on sector rotation** currently available. It combines depth, practicality, and personal insight in a way that's both approachable and actionable. If you're serious about learning sector rotation or upgrading your investing strategy, this book should be on your desk—not your shelf.

Art of Investing 5th Edition

⭐⭐⭐⭐ ½ (4.5/5)

Art of Investing: 5th Edition is a **must-read** for investors who want to actively manage their portfolios and seek strategies beyond passive investing. Tony Pow presents a well-researched, experience-backed guide that can help investors navigate market cycles and maximize returns. If you are looking for an investing book that combines data, strategy, and personal insights, this one is worth adding to your library.

Sector Rotation 5th Edition, one of my top sellers. Your book is an impressive and valuable resource for investors interested in sector rotation. It stands out for its depth, practical strategies, and real-world examples.

Rating: 9.5/10

Sector Rotation: 5th Edition is arguably **the most complete book on sector rotation** currently available. It combines depth, practicality, and personal insight in a way that's both approachable and actionable. If you're serious about learning sector rotation or upgrading your investing strategy, this book should be on your desk—not your shelf.

Using Finviz 5th Edition, one of my best sellers. *Using Finviz 5th Edition* is a valuable resource for investors seeking to leverage Finviz.com effectively. Its blend of foundational principles, advanced strategies, and modern tools like AI makes it versatile. However, readers should critically assess self-reported success and adapt strategies to current market conditions. The book's reference-style format encourages revisiting chapters as skills evolve.

Recommendation:
Ideal for retail investors with basic market knowledge aiming to deepen their technical and strategic expertise. Pair with real-time market data and independent research for best results.
Rating: ★★★★☆ (4/5)
A thorough, practical guide with minor caveats around self-promotion and data timeliness

Using Fidelity 5th Edition

⭐⭐⭐⭐ ½ (4.5/5)

Using Fidelity: 5th Edition is an excellent guide for Fidelity customers looking to leverage the platform's research tools and advanced features. It provides in-depth investment strategies that have historically outperformed the market. While the book may feel dense at times, its wealth of knowledge makes it a highly valuable resource for serious investors. If you're looking to enhance your investing skills using Fidelity's platform, this book is a must-read.

Investing Lessons: successes and plunders

Offers a comprehensive and insightful look into investing strategies, experiences,

Best Stocks to Buy for 2025 is an excellent resource for investors seeking **data-driven, well-researched stock recommendations**. Your **historical performance, emphasis on market timing, and risk management strategies** set it apart.
However, **a more structured format, better visuals, and slight content trimming**
would improve readability and engagement.
and lessons learned over the years.

Profit from Bull, Bear, and Sideway Markets

It is a valuable resource for traders seeking a versatile toolkit. Its structured advice on adapting to market shifts, coupled with robust risk management frameworks, makes it a worthwhile read. While not without minor flaws—particularly in depth and modernity—it succeeds in delivering actionable insights across market cycles. Recommended for intermediate traders aiming to build resilience in volatile environments.
Rating: 4/5 (Balanced coverage and practicality offset by occasional superficiality and dated content in older editions).

Profitable Covered calls
Overall Rating:
⭐ ⭐ ⭐ ⭐ (4/5) – A valuable resource for covered call strategies, especially for investors who want a mix of personal experience and market insights. With better editing and organization, it could be a top-tier investing guide.

Shorting stocks and ETFs
Final Verdict:
Your book is an excellent resource for intermediate to advanced

investors looking to deepen their knowledge of short selling and market timing. With some refinements in structure and editing, it could be even more impactful. Rated at 4/5.

Artificial Intelligence Investing. Tony Pow's book, *Artificial Intelligence Investing*, is a detailed guide for investors looking to capitalize on the AI revolution. It combines practical investment strategies with insights into the future of AI and its impact on various sectors. The author's emphasis on risk management, market timing, and long-term value investing makes this book a valuable resource for both novice and seasoned investors.

Profitable Covered Call. Overall Rating:
⭐ ⭐ ⭐ ⭐ (4/5) – A valuable resource for covered call strategies, especially for investors who want a mix of personal experience and market insights. With better editing and organization, it could be a top-tier investing guide.

Best stocks to buy for 2025

The current book is "Best stocks for 2025" in this series.
https://www.amazon.com/dp/B0D2459JDT
If available, future books could be titled "for 2026" around Dec. 20, 2025).

If the sales of my books in this series were based on past performances, I should have sold many books, but obviously not.

Book	Stocks	Return[3]	Ann.	Beat RSP by[1]
Best stocks to buy for 2024	8	46%	48%	132%
Best stocks to buy for 2023	8	36%	36%	290%
Best stocks to buy for 2022	10[6]	4%	4%	153%[7]
Best Stocks to buy as of July, 2021[4]	8	5%	13%	487%
Best Stocks for 2021 2nd Edition	10	42%[4]	52%	220%
Best Stocks for 2021	4	29%	44%	118%
Best Stocks to Buy from Aug, 2020	14	45%	45%	3%[5]
Avg.	9	34%	40%	208%[2]

Here is the detail:
https://tonyp4idea.blogspot.com/2024/12/best-stocks-to-buy-for-2025.html

---

Art of Investing

Art of Investing 5th Edition consisting of 15 books in 1. Besides saving money and your digital shelve space, it gives you quick reference and concentration on the topic you're currently interested in. It covers most investing topics in investing excluding speculative investing such as currency trading and day trading. It has over 600 pages (6*9), about the size of two investing books of average size. If you have any of my investing books less than 200 pages, this is the one for your **next reading.**

The 15 books

Book No.	Amazon.com
1	Simple techniques
2	Finding Stocks
3	Evaluating Stocks
4	Scoring Stocks
5	Trading Stocks
6	Market Timing
7	Strategies
8	Sector Rotation
9	Insider Trading
10	Penny Stocks & Micro Cap
11	Momentum Investing
12	Dividend Investing
13	Technical Analysis
14	Investing Ideas
15	Buffettology

The book links are subject to change without notice.

"How to be a billionaire" is for beginners and couch potatoes, who can use the advanced features of this book in the simplest and less time-consuming techniques. Most advance users can skip this section unless they want to use some of the short cuts described.

We start with the basic books Finding Stocks, Evaluate Stocks, Trading Stocks and Market Timing. You can select and start with one of the many styles and strategies in investing such as swing trading and top-down strategy. Many tools are described in other books such as ETFs, technical analysis, covered calls and trading plan.

Many books start with "Why" to lure you to read more and are followed by "How" and then the theory behind the book.
If the book you're reading is beneficial to you, imagine how it would with 850 pages.

Most readers' comments are on "Debunk the Myths in Investing", which this book is originally based on. As of 2018, I did not know any of the commentators on my books.

"I skipped ahead to his chapter book 14 (of "Complete the Art of Investing"), Investment Advice just to get a feel of his writing style. His research is phenomenal and doesn't overwhelm with big words or catchy "sales-like" tactics.

I truly believe this ordinary man, Mr. Tony Pow, has a gift of explaining his experience as an investor without the bull crap of trying to make you buy his stuff. He seemingly just wants to share his knowledge, tips, and clarity of definitions for the kind of folks like me who want to understand something FIRST before jumping in with emotions of trying to make a boat load of money. I like the technical analysis side he brings.

Mr. Tony Pow talks about hidden gems in his book; well....quite frankly, he is a hidden gem. Thank you and I will also post my comments about this author to my Facebook page!" – JB on this book.

"Excellent book, recommend to all investors... great knowledge. It has fine-tuned my investing strategies... Your book is hard to set aside, as I read it all the time learning good techniques and analysis of stocks, ETF... Since I purchased your book in March, I have underlined, highlighted and placed tabs on top of pages for quick reference." – Aileron on this book.

"Tony, I just finished reading your 2nd edition. It's my pleasure to report that I found it most interesting. You're welcome to use this blurb if you like:

Debunk the Myths in Investing is an all-encompassing look at not only the most salient factors influencing markets and investors, but also a from-the-trenches look at many of the misconceptions and mistakes too many investors make. Reading this book may save not only time and aggravation but money as well!"

Joseph Shaefer, CEO, Stanford Wealth Management LLC.

"Tony, Great work!" from James and Chris, who are portfolio managers.

"'Debunk the Myths in Investing' is a comprehensive book on investing that deals with many aspects of this tense profession in which with a lot of knowledge and a bit of luck (or vice versa) one can greatly benefit...

Therefore 'Debunk the Myths in Investing' is an interesting book that on its 500 pages offer a lot of knowledge related to investing world and many practical advice, so I can recommend its reading if you're interested in this topic."
- Denis Vukosav, Top 500 Reviewers at Amazon.com.

"490 pages (Debunk) of a genius's ranting and hypothesis with various theories throughout, written light-heartedly with ample doses of humor...Yes, the myth of not being able to profitably time the market is BUSTED...

One might ask... Why is he giving away the results of his hard-earned research for only $20? He states that his children are not interested in investing and wants to share his efforts with the world." - Abe Agoda.

"Excellent book, recommend to all investors... great knowledge. It has fine-tuned my investing strategies... Your book is hard to set aside, as I read it all the time learning good techniques and analysis of stocks, ETF... Since I purchased your book in March, I have underlined, highlighted and placed tabs on top of pages for quick reference." - Aileron on this book.

"Great stuff, Tony. It's great to meet experienced traders such as yourself. I had a browse through the book and think your method is a little more refined than mine."

"Your strategy is very rules based and solid. I sometimes envy people who have developed something like this."

Making 50% in one month

I claim to have the best one-month performance ever for recommending 8 or more stocks without using options and leverage. My following return is 57% in a month or 621% annualized. They are slightly different as I calculated the average from the averages of three different accounts. The average buy date is 12/26/18 and the "current date" is 01/28/19.

The performance may not be repeated. I will use the same screen for the coming years and even the expected 10% (or 120% annualized) is very good.

I used the same screen for searching stock candidates. I spent a total of about 20 hours from Dec. 15, 2018 to Jan. 5, 2019.

Stock	Buy Price	Sold or Current Price	Buy date	Sold or Current date	Profit %	Profit % Ann.	Status
CHK	2.13	2.99	01/03/09	01/18/19	40%	982%	Sold
MNK	16.41	21.45	01/03/19	01/25/19	31%	510%	Sold
MNK	16.43	21.45	01/03/19	01/25/19	31%	507%	Sold
NNBR	5.68	8.58	12/26/18	01/28/19	51%	565%	
NNBR	5.72	8.58	12/26/18	01/28/19	66%	727%	
ESTE	4.35	6.45	12/26/18	01/18/19	48%	766%	Sold
LCI	4.61	8.29	12/21/18	01/28/19	80%	767%	
MDR	8.01	9.13	01/08/19	01/28/19	14%	255%	
YRCW	3.29	5.78	12/21/18	01/28/19	76%	727%	
YRCW	3.26	5.78	12/21/18	01/28/19	77%	742%	
ASRT	3.56	4.18	12/26/18	01/28/19	17%	193%	
UTCC	7.13	11.00	12/26/18	01/28/19	54%	600%	
YRCW	2.92	5.78	12/26/18	01/28/19	98%	1083%	

Best one-year return

I claim to have the best-performed article in Seeking Alpha history, an investing site, for recommending 15 or more stocks in one year after the publish date without using options and leverage.

https://seekingalpha.com/article/1095671-amazing-returns-velti-alcatel-lucent-alpha-natural-resources

Appendix 2: Reviews by the unbiased AI

Many thanks to the most unbiased reviews by AI. My following books were rated from 8 to 9.5 out of 10. Recently, DeepSeek does not review books over a specific size.

I accept all suggestions. However, I did repeat a few important concepts, so the reader does not have to waste time in searching for them. Some examples are older for a good reason. For example, if I did not use the market crash of 2000, I only had one market crash to illustrate. It is always better to follow the winners, though I have included my blunders in investing.

Review of "Art of Investing 5th Edition " 9/10

ChatGPT Review

Overall Impression:
Art of Investing: 5th Edition is an extensive, well-structured guide designed for investors of all levels. With over 600 pages, it offers a deep dive into investing strategies, market timing, risk management, and stock selection. The book blends personal experience with data-driven techniques, making it both informative and practical.

Strengths:

☑ **Comprehensive Coverage** – The book spans 16 "mini-books," covering everything from beginner investing techniques to advanced stock scoring, market cycles, and sector rotation strategies. It even includes guidance on artificial intelligence in investing.

☑ **Proven Strategies** – The author shares his own investment successes, highlighting methods that have consistently outperformed the S&P 500. His use of sector rotation, fundamental analysis, and market timing offers valuable insights.

☑ **Practicality & Accessibility** – The book is structured as a reference manual rather than a linear read, allowing investors to jump to relevant sections. It also includes actionable advice, checklists, and step-by-step guides.

☑ **Personal Insights & Humor** – The inclusion of personal anecdotes, humor, and lighthearted "fillers" makes the book more engaging than a traditional investing manual.

☑ **Use of Free Tools** – The book extensively references resources like Finviz, Fidelity, and ETFdb, making sophisticated analysis accessible to retail investors without costly subscriptions.

Areas for Improvement:

- **Length & Density** – At over 600 pages, the book is packed with information, which can be overwhelming for beginners. A more concise version or a summary section for each chapter could improve readability.
- **Editing & Formatting** – Some sections could benefit from tighter editing to improve flow and readability. The humor and filler content, while entertaining, might feel excessive for readers looking for a purely analytical approach.
- **Market Timing Debate** – While the book provides strong evidence supporting market timing strategies, some traditional investors may find this approach debatable, as it contradicts the "buy and hold" philosophy endorsed by many long-term investors.

Final Verdict:

⭐ ⭐ ⭐ ⭐ ½ (4.5/5)

Art of Investing: 5th Edition is a must-read for investors who want to actively manage their portfolios and seek strategies beyond passive investing. Tony Pow presents a well-researched, experience-backed guide that can help investors navigate market cycles and maximize returns. If you are looking for an investing book that combines data, strategy, and personal insights, this one is worth adding to your library.

DeepSeek Review

Your book, *Art of Investing 5th Edition*, is a comprehensive and practical guide that caters to investors of all levels, from beginners to advanced fund managers. Here's a review based on the content provided:

Strengths:

1. **Comprehensive Coverage:**
   - The book covers a wide range of topics, from basic investment strategies to advanced techniques like sector rotation, market timing, and insider trading. It's structured into 16 interconnected "books," each focusing on specific aspects of investing, making it both a reference guide and a practical manual.

2. **Proven Strategies:**
   - You share your personal investment strategies and techniques, many of which have been proven to outperform the market. For example, your sector rotation strategy has yielded returns exceeding five times your initial investment, and your stock recommendations have consistently beaten the S&P 500.

3. **Practical Tools and Resources:**
   - The book emphasizes the use of free or low-cost tools like Finviz, Fidelity, and ETFdb, making it accessible to

retail investors. You also provide step-by-step instructions on how to use these tools effectively.

4. **Risk Management:**
   o You stress the importance of risk management, advocating for stop-loss orders, diversification, and avoiding leverage for beginners. This is crucial for long-term success in investing.

5. **Market Timing:**
   o Your market timing techniques, particularly the use of SMA (Simple Moving Averages) and RSI (Relative Strength Index), are well-explained and have been effective in avoiding major market downturns.

6. **Personal Insights:**
   o You share your personal successes and mistakes, making the content relatable and actionable. This transparency adds credibility and helps readers learn from your experiences.

7. **Focus on Education:**
   o The book encourages readers to practice with paper trading and provides practical exercises. This hands-on approach is beneficial for beginners who need to build confidence before investing real money.

8. **AI Integration:**
   o The inclusion of AI tools like ChatGPT and DeepSeek for stock analysis and market predictions is forward-thinking, though you caution readers about the limitations of outdated databases.

Weaknesses:

1. **Dense and Lengthy:**
   o While the book is comprehensive, its length (770 pages) and density might be overwhelming for some readers, especially beginners. The sheer volume of information could make it difficult to digest in one go.

2. **Outdated Data:**
   o Some of the examples and data, particularly those related to specific stocks or market conditions, may become outdated quickly. While you advise readers to focus on the rationale behind the examples rather than the specific stocks, this could still be a limitation.

3. **Complexity for Beginners:**
   o Although you provide beginner-friendly sections, some of the advanced techniques (e.g., short selling, momentum investing) might still be too complex for novice investors. The book could benefit from more simplified explanations or additional beginner-focused content.

4. **Over-Reliance on Specific Tools:**
   o The book heavily relies on specific tools like Finviz and Fidelity. While these are excellent resources, readers who prefer other platforms might find it challenging to adapt the strategies to their preferred tools.

5. **AI Limitations:**
   o While the integration of AI is innovative, the reliance on AI tools like ChatGPT and DeepSeek comes with the caveat that their databases may not be up-to-date. This could lead to outdated or inaccurate recommendations, which you acknowledge but could be a concern for readers.

Overall Impression:

Art of Investing 5th Edition is a valuable resource for anyone looking to improve their investment skills. It's particularly well-suited for intermediate to advanced investors who are familiar with the basics and are looking to refine their strategies. The book's strength lies in its practical, actionable advice and the author's willingness to share personal insights and proven techniques.

However, beginners might find the book overwhelming due to its length and the complexity of some topics. Additionally, while the inclusion of AI tools is innovative, readers should be cautious about relying too heavily on them due to potential data limitations.

Final Verdict:

Overall, *Art of Investing 5th Edition* is a solid, well-researched, and practical guide that offers a wealth of information for investors. It's a must-read for those who are serious about improving their investment acumen and achieving long-term financial success. However, beginners may need to take it slow and focus on the foundational sections before diving into the more advanced strategies.

Rating: 4.5/5

"Using Finviz 5th Editon" and "Using Fidelity 5th Edition"
are similar to "Art of Investing" with changes specific to the topic.

"Using Finviz" is rated 8/10: TonyP4Idea: Review of "Using Finviz 5th Edition"

"Using Fidelity is rated   9/10: TonyP4Idea: Review of "Using Fidelity 5th Edition"

Review of " Best stocks to buy for 2025"

Your book, **Best Stocks to Buy for 2025 (Note:** *the next book is "2026")*, is a highly detailed and data-driven investment guide that builds on the success of previous editions. Here's a structured review of its strengths and areas for improvement.

Strengths:
1. Proven Track Record
- You provide historical performance data from previous editions, showing that your stock picks have consistently outperformed the RSP (equal-weight S&P 500 ETF).
- The book highlights an average outperformance of over 200% across past editions, reinforcing credibility.

2. Comprehensive Stock Selection Strategy
- The book includes a **Primary List** for long-term investing and multiple **sub-lists** for short-term trading (3-month and 6-month holding periods).
- Uses fundamental metrics, Finviz screening, and AI-generated stock ideas for diverse stock selection.

3. Practical Investing Insights
- Explores short-term and long-term strategies, including momentum trades and market timing approaches.
- Discusses stop-loss techniques, trailing stops, and how to protect profits effectively.

4. Market Timing & Risk Management
- Includes detailed insights on market cycles, bear market indicators, and strategies to hedge against downturns.
- The book's emphasis on **when** to invest (market timing) rather than just **what** to buy adds significant value.

5. Educational Value
- Goes beyond stock recommendations by covering fundamental analysis, technical indicators (Bollinger Bands, RSI, MACD), and investment psychology.
- Offers a structured approach, making it suitable for both beginners and seasoned investors.

Areas for Improvement:
1. Organization & Readability
- The book is **very dense** (over 375 pages), which can be overwhelming.
- Consider **streamlining the layout** by adding bullet points, clearer section breaks, and summaries at the end of each chapter.
2. More Visual Aids

- While data tables are helpful, adding **more charts, graphs, and stock performance visuals** would make complex ideas easier to grasp.

3. Conciseness
- Some sections, particularly on past performance, are **repetitive**.
- Shortening these parts or summarizing key findings in a table format could improve readability.

4. More Case Studies & Examples
- Including **detailed breakdowns of past successful trades** would enhance the learning experience.
- A step-by-step example of how a selected stock performed over time, including entry and exit points, could be valuable.

Final Thoughts:

Best Stocks to Buy for 2025 is an excellent resource for investors seeking **data-driven, well-researched stock recommendations.** Your **historical performance, emphasis on market timing, and risk management strategies** set it apart.

However, **a more structured format, better visuals, and slight content trimming** would improve readability and engagement.

"I have read your book : "Stocks To Buy 2024" and it's excellent. I keep it close to me and read it sometimes to remind me some principles. It's in my top 5 and I've read more than a hundred ones." – Eric, 3/23/2025

Review of "Sector Rotation 5th Edition" rated 9.5

Overview

Tony Pow's *Sector Rotation: 5th Edition* is an exceptionally thorough and practical guide that stands out in the crowded field of investment literature. With over 500 pages and 21 distinct strategies, this book offers a deep dive into the theory and execution of sector rotation, drawing on the author's decades of hands-on experience and real-world performance.

Strengths

☑ Unmatched Strategy Depth

- The book covers **21 sector rotation strategies**, far surpassing competing titles that usually offer only one or two.
- It includes approaches ranging from simple ETF-and-cash rotation for beginners to advanced momentum, contrarian, insider, and macroeconomic strategies.

☑ Proven Performance

- Pow backs his strategies with concrete results—including a **fivefold portfolio growth** through sector rotation, and outperformance of the S&P 500 by nearly **184%** across his recent book series.
- Specific calls, like recommending SMCI with a 272% return (Tony: my first twelve bagger at its peak), and oil at the 2016 bottom, establish his credibility.

☑ Tailored for All Investor Levels

- The book includes dedicated sections for beginners, intermediate, and advanced investors.
- Each strategy is labeled with difficulty and practical tips, helping readers choose based on experience and time commitment.

☑ Educational + Entertaining

- Pow intersperses serious content with humor, real-life anecdotes, and fillers to lighten the tone—creating an educational yet engaging read.
- AI-assisted summaries and commentary from tools like ChatGPT and DeepSeek help distill complex topics into actionable insights.

☑ Practical Tools and Real-World Application

- Heavy use of **Finviz, Fidelity, and ETF databases** for real-time sector evaluation.
- Uses technical indicators like RSI(14), SMA, MACD in a digestible, non-overwhelming way.
- Includes links to video tutorials and online references to support readers using digital versions.

Areas for Improvement

⚠ Length and Redundancy

- At over 500 pages, the book can be overwhelming. While repetition helps reinforce concepts, some ideas are restated more often than necessary.

⚠ Flow and Navigation

- The structure is more reference-like than linear. Beginners might benefit from a "quick-start roadmap" or flowchart to guide initial reading.

⚠ Design and Formatting

- Some visual elements (e.g., charts and tables) may not render well on small e-reader screens. The author does note this and offers workarounds.

Noteworthy Features

- **AI Integration:** The book leverages ChatGPT and DeepSeek to review, polish, and even write several sections—showcasing how investors can benefit from AI in content creation and market analysis.
- **Humility and Honesty:** The author shares not only successes but also missed opportunities and mistakes, offering readers real insight into risk management and psychological pitfalls.
- **Top-Down & Bottom-Up Coverage:** The mix of macroeconomic cycle theories (e.g., sector sensitivity to interest rates and politics) with micro-level stock selection tools makes this comprehensive.

Final Verdict

▨ Rating: 9.5/10

Sector Rotation: 5th Edition is arguably **the most complete book on sector rotation** currently available. It combines depth, practicality, and personal insight in a way that's both approachable and actionable. If you're serious about learning sector rotation or upgrading your investing strategy, this book should be on your desk—not your shelf.

Review of "Your first dollar for smart investing "

ChatGPT

✅ Strengths

1. Clear Purpose and Audience

- The book clearly targets beginners and delivers on that goal.

- Your tone is friendly, practical, and non-patronizing — perfect for newcomers.

- It positions the "first dollar" wisely — focusing on security, simplicity, and learning.

2. Actionable Advice

- You emphasize using ETFs like VOO/SPY, avoiding leverage, setting stop losses, and using practical tools like Finviz, which are great entry-level practices.

- The step-by-step guidance for evaluating stocks, ETF analysis, and market timing is simplified but effective.

- Including your personal recommendations, tools, and specific links (e.g., YouTube, Fidelity, Finviz) gives readers clear next steps.

3. Unique Selling Points

- Priced at $1, it truly aligns with the concept: smart investing starts with smart spending.

- The integration of AI (like ChatGPT and DeepSeek) as co-editors and advisors is forward-looking and distinguishes this from traditional investing books.

- Many sections feel like a hybrid of personal coaching and DIY investing — a rare tone in finance books.

▓ Final Thoughts

This book is well-aligned for its purpose and price:

- **Approachable, practical**, and **authentic**.

- A **useful primer** that competes well with free articles or $20+ beginner guides.

Final Thoughts from DeepSeek:

Tony Pow's book delivers on its promise: a **budget-friendly, no-nonsense guide** for investing newcomers. Its strengths lie in simplicity and actionable steps, though it lacks depth for seasoned readers. The AI-assisted content is a novelty, but the real value is in the foundational advice—perfect for someone investing their "first dollar."

Rating: ★★★★☆ (4/5)
Recommendation: Highly

Reviewd on 5/28/2025

Review of "Momentum Investing 3rd Edition "

Strengths:
1. **Extensive Data & Performance Tracking** – You provide a thorough history of your momentum stock trades, including real-world examples and performance analysis, which adds credibility.
2. **Diverse Momentum Strategies** – You break momentum investing into multiple strategies, catering to different holding periods and risk tolerances.
3. **Sector Rotation & Market Timing** – The book successfully integrates sector rotation and market timing to enhance momentum strategies.
4. **Practical Implementation** – Step-by-step guides on using platforms like Finviz, Seeking Alpha, and Fidelity make it easy for readers to apply the strategies.
5. **Personal Investment Experience** – Your personal trading history and transparent performance records provide valuable lessons for readers.

Final Verdict:
This is an in-depth and practical guide for momentum investors, backed by real-world experience.

Review of "Using profitable investment sites" rated 8

Strengths

Comprehensive Coverage – The book provides in-depth discussions on various investment platforms, strategies, and techniques, covering fundamental and technical analysis, sector rotation, market timing, and more.

Practical Insights – You include personal investment experiences and strategies, making the content relatable and actionable for readers.

Structured for Different Investors – It caters to beginner, intermediate, and advanced investors, helping readers navigate content at their level.

Focus on Market Timing & Sector Rotation – These strategies can be useful for those looking to enhance returns beyond standard buy-and-hold approaches.

Use of Free and Paid Investment Tools – The book effectively highlights how to leverage platforms like Barron's, Finviz, and Seeking Alpha for research.

Final Verdict

Rating: 4/5

Your book is a **valuable resource for self-directed investors**, particularly those interested in using online tools for research and market timing. With tighter editing and better visual organization, it could become an even more **impactful investment guide.**

Review of "Investing successes and blunders"

Strengths:
1. **Practical Experience:** Your personal investing experiences, both successes and mistakes, add authenticity and credibility. Readers can learn from real-life examples rather than just theoretical concepts.
2. **Data-Driven Approach:** Your detailed performance tracking of stock picks and strategies over multiple years demonstrates a commitment to rigorous analysis.
3. **Market Timing Insights:** The emphasis on simple market timing techniques and avoiding common pitfalls, such as emotional investing and overreliance on government policies, is valuable.
4. **Sector-Specific Insights:** Your discussion of various market sectors, including AI, real estate, bonds, and commodities, helps readers understand different investment opportunities.

Risk Management: Your explanations of calculated vs. blind risks, the importance of diversification, and strategies like stop-loss orders are useful for investors at all levels.

Appendix 3 - Our window to the investing world

The paperback version of this chapter can be found in the following link.
http://ebmyth.blogspot.com/2013/11/web-sites.html

- **General**
  Wikipedia / Investopedia /Yahoo!Finance / MarketWatch / Cnnfn / Morningstar /CNBC / Bloomberg / WSJ / Barron's / Motley Fool / TheStreet
- **Evaluate stocks**
  Finviz / SeekingAlpha / MSN Money / Zacks / Daily Finance / ADR / Fidelity / Earnings Impact / OpenInsider / NYSE / NASDAQ / SEC / SEC for 10K and 10Q (quarterly) reports required to file for listed stocks in major exchanges.
- **Charts**
  BigCharts / FreeStockCharts / StockCharts /
- **Screens**
  Yahoo!Finance / Finviz / CNBC / Morningstar /
- **Besides stocks**
  123Jump / Hoover's Online / FINRA Bond Market Data / REIT / Commodity Futures / Option Industry
- **Vendors**
  AAII / Zacks / IBD / GuruFocus / VectorVest / Fidelity / Interactive Brokers / Merrill Lynch /
- **Economy.**
  Econday / EcoconStats / Federal Reserve / Economist /
- **Misc.**
  Dow Jones Indices / Russell / Wilshire / IRS / Wikinvest / ETF Database / ETF Trends / Nolo (estate planning) / AARP /

Appendix 4 - ETFs / Mutual Funds

What is an ETF

ETFs have basic differences from mutual funds: 1. Lower management expenses, 2. Trade ETFs same as stocks, and 3. Usually more diversified but not more selective than the related mutual funds such as NOBL vs FRDPX.

The major classifications of ETFs are 1. Simulating an index such as SPY, QQQ and DIA, 2. Simulating a sector such as XLE and SOXX, 3. Simulating an asset class such as GLD and SLV, 4. Simulating a country or a group of countries such as EWC and FXI, 5. Managed by a manager(s) such as ARKK, 6. Betting a market or sector to go down such as SH and PSQ, and 7. Leveraged (not recommended for beginners).

Fidelity: Index ETFs (https://www.fidelity.com/etfs/overview).

Wikipedia on ETF (http://en.wikipedia.org/wiki/Exchange-traded_fund).

List of ETFs
ETF database (Recommended): http://etfdb.com/
ETF Bloomberg: http://www.bloomberg.com/markets/etfs/
ETF Trends: http://www.etftrends.com/
A list of ETFs. Seeking Alpha.
http://etf.stock-encyclopedia.com/category/)
A list of contra ETFs (or bear ETFs)
http://www.tradermike.net/inverse-short-etfs-bearish-etf-funds/
Misc.: ETFGuide, ETFReplay
Fidelity low-cost index funds:
https://www.youtube.com/watch?v=zpKi4_IJvlY
Fidelity Annuity funds with performance data.
http://fundresearch.fidelity.com/annuities/category-performance-annual-total-returns-quarterly/FPRAI?refann=005
ETFs vs mutual funds;
https://www.youtube.com/watch?v=Vmz0CzlQvHk
Three ETFs: https://www.youtube.com/watch?v=MVi2RhpffuU

Other resources
Most subscription services offer research on ETFs. IBD has a strategy dedicated to ETFs and so does AAII to name a couple. Seeking Alpha has extensive resources for ETF including an ETF screener and investing ideas. So is ETFdb.

Not all ETFs are created equal
Check their performances and their expenses.

When to use or not to use ETFs

I prefer sector mutual funds in some industries, as they have many bad stocks such as drug industry, banks, miners and insurers. Most mutual funds cannot time the market.

When you believe a sector is heading up (or contra ETF for heading down), but you do not have time to do research on specific stocks, buy an ETF for the sector; it is same for the market.

Half ETF

Taking out half of the stocks that score below the average in an index ETF could beat the same full ETF itself. I call it HETF (half the ETF). You heard it here first. After a decade, at least one company has a similar product.

To illustrate, sort the expected P/E (not including stocks with negative earnings) in ascending order and only include the stocks on the first half. Add more fundamental metrics. It will take a few minutes.

Disadvantages of ETFs
- When you have two stocks in a sector ETF one good one and one bad one, the ETF treats them the same. Stock pickers would buy the one that has a better appreciation potential.
- Sometimes the return could be misleading due to stock rotation. To illustrate this, on August 29, 2012, SHLD was replaced by LYB in a sector fund. SHLD was down by 4% and LYB was up by 4% primarily due to the switch. Unless you sell and buy at the right time (which is impossible), your return would not match the ETF's returns due to the replacement.
- Ensure the performance matches the corresponding index; it is hard due to excluding dividends.

Advantages of ETFs
- We have demonstrated that you can beat the market by using market timing. Between 2000 and Nov., 2013, you only exit and reenter the market 3 times and the result is astonishing.
- It is easy to rotate a sector vs. buying/selling all of the stocks in this sector. Rotating a sector is the same as trading a stock.

- The risk is spread out, and your portfolio is diversified especially for a market ETF or buying three or more ETFs in different sectors.
- Periodically the bad stocks in most funds are replaced by better stocks.
- Eliminate the time in researching stocks.

Leveraged ETFs

I do not recommend them. Some are 2x, 3x and even higher. They're too risky for beginners. However, when you are very sure or your tested strategy has very low drawdown, you may want to use them to improve performance. Most leveraged ETFs and contra ETFs have higher fees.

My basic ETF tables

I include some contra ETFs, mutual funds and Fidelity's annuity. Some of these may be interesting to you. Most Vanguard's ETFs have lower fees.

ETFs and funds come and go. Some ideas and classifications are my own interpretation. Refer to ETFdb for updated information. Not responsible for any error. Check out the ETF or fund before you take any action.

I prefer VFINX over SPY for the lower fees; both simulate the S&P 500 index. The stocks in the ETF can be either equally weighted or weighted by market caps. The latter is more like using momentum strategy, as the rising stocks usually have larger market caps. The index usually kicks out some poor-performing stocks and replaced them with better stocks. These ETFs are suited for long-term investing without constant reviews.

Table by market cap:

Category	ETF	Mutual Funds	Fidelity's Annuity	Contra ETF	Alternate
Size:					
Large Cap	DIA			DOG	
	SPY			SH	VOO VFINX RSP FXAIX
	QQQ			PSQ	FNCMX
	RYH				
Blend	IWD	BEQGX			
Growth	SPYG	FBGRX			FSPGX

Value	SPYV	DOGGX			FLCOX
Dividend	NOBL	FRDPX			
	VYM				
Mid Cap			FNBSC	MYY	
Blend	MDY	VSEQX			
Growth		STDIX			
		BPTRX			
Value		FSMVX			
Small Cap			FPRGC	SBB	FSSNX
Blend	IWM	HDPSX			
Growth		PRDSX			FECGX
Value		SKSEX			FISVX
Micro	IWC				
Multi					
Blend		VDEOX			
Growth		VHCOX			
Value		TCLCX			
Total					FSKAX VTI
Bond					
Long Term (20)	VLV	BTTTX		TBF	
Mid Term (7 – 10)	VCIT	FSTGX			
Short Term (1 – 3 yrs.)	VCSH	THOPX			
Total	BOND	PONDX			
Corp Invest Grade	VCIT	NTHEX			
High Yield (junk)	PHB	SPHIX			
Muni	MUB	Check state			
Special situation					
Buy back	PKW				

Table by sectors:

Sector	ETF	Mutual Funds	Fidelity's Annuity
Banking[1]		FSRBK	
Regional	IAT		
Biotech	IBB	FBIOX	
	XBI	Large	

Consumer Dis.	XLY	FSCPX	FVHAC
Consumer Staple	XLP	FDFAX	FCSAC
Defense + Aero	PPA		
Finance	KIE	FIDSX	FONNC
	IYF		
Energy	XLE	FSENX	FJLLC
Energy Service		FSESX	
Farm	DBA		
Gold	GLD	FSAGX	BAR
Gold Miner	GDX	VGPMX	
Health Care	IYH	FSPHX	FPDRC
	VHT	VGHCX	
House Builder	ITB	FSHOX	
Industrial	IYJ	FCYIX	FBALC
Material	VAW	FSDPX	GSG
	IYM		
Natural Gas	UNG		
Oil	USO		
Oil Service	OIH	FSESX	
Oil Exploration	XOP		
Real Estate	VNQ	FRIFX	FFWLC
REIT	VNQ		
Retail	RTH	FSRPX	
	XRT		
Regional bank	KRE	FSRBX	
Semi Conduct	SMH		
Software	XSW	FSCSX	
	IGV		
Technology	XLK	FSPTX	FYENC
	FDN	FBSOX	
		ROGSX	
Telecomm.	VOX	FSTCX	FVTAC
Transport	XTN		
	IYT		
Utilities	XLU	FSUTX	FKMSC
Wireless		FWRLX	

Footnote. [1] Also check Finance.

Table by countries outside the USA:

Country	ETF	Mutual Funds	Fidelity's Annuity	Alternate
Australia	EWA			
Brazil	EWZ			
Canada	EWC	FICDX		
China	FXI	FHKCX		
EAFE	EFA			
Emerging	VWO	FEMEX	FEMAC	FPADX
Europe	VGK	FIEUX		
Global	KXI	PGVFX		
Greece	GREK			
India	INDY	MINDX		
Indonesia	EIDO			
Latin America	ILF	FLATX		
Nordic		FNORX		
Hong Kong	EWH			
Japan	EWJ	FJPNX		
S. Africa	EZA			
S. Korea	EWY	MAKOX		
Singapore	EWS			
Taiwan	EWT			
Turkey	TUR			
United Kingdom	EWU			
Foreign:				
Combination				
Intern. Div.	IDV			FTIHX
Small Cap	SCZ			
Value	EFV			
Europe	VGK			

Appendix 5 - Links

The following may be repeated from the articles and it is for your convenience. To illustrate, Under YouTube (or Investopedia), search "Finviz". Some links have permanent values such as most articles from Wikipedia and Investopedia. Others reflect current events such as the current market. Learn from them and act when the current events have similar descriptions. For the printed versions and updated links, enter the following in your browser: https://tonyp4idea.blogspot.com/2023/02/links-in-my-books.html

Beginners

Common mistakes: https://www.youtube.com/watch?v=zkNueyFs8zQ

Best Vanguard ETFs https://www.youtube.com/watch?v=mSEyghlZchQ

Buy stocks/ETFs: https://www.youtube.com/watch?v=4vjkeC_4EmU

Screener

Finviz https://www.youtube.com/watch?v=cHNUMPgEYGY

Recommended YouTube: https://www.youtube.com/watch?v=CJoN7wLfWNo
PEG: http://en.wikipedia.org/wiki/PEG_ratio
Short %:
http://www.investopedia.com/university/shortselling/shortselling1.asp#axzz2LNDvpemo

Openinsider:	http://www.openinsider.com/
Finviz:	http://Finviz.com/
terms:	http://www.Finviz.com/help/screener.ashx
Insider Cow:	http://www.insidercow.com/
Current Ratio:	http://en.wikipedia.org/wiki/Current_ratio
Cash Flow:	https://www.youtube.com/watch?v=1v8hRZ36--c
Balance sheet:	https://www.youtube.com/watch?v=DZjU0CHKyV4

How to find quality stocks.
http://seekingalpha.com/article/2381395-how-to-identify-quality-stocks-and-is-there-really-alpha-to-be-had

Investing strategies

Inflation: https://www.youtube.com/watch?v=Zpthvpy3UKg\

Swing: https://www.youtube.com/watch?v=C9EQkA7uVU8
          https://www.youtube.com/watch?v=a_wpfSXRSjo
https://www.youtube.com/watch?v=M8sNMhPJlN

Momentum: https://www.youtube.com/watch?v=PpUlOyZrl9
Penny stocks: https://www.youtube.com/watch?v=u7xZ3kF62u4

Scanning https://www.youtube.com/watch?v=7iZpWmwBheI

Peter lynch 2023: https://www.youtube.com/watch?v=CK1AkVVVXu8

Charlie: **https://www.youtube.com/watch?v=8g2B6QJ2FEc**
Dividend ETFs: https://www.youtube.com/watch?v=64NEiyoNBIM

- Innovative   sectors:
https://www.youtube.com/watch?v=LI1hMX8qtHg

Trading stocks
Beginners: https://www.youtube.com/watch?v=aod3cyUEu4k
Covered call https://www.youtube.com/watch?v=dzMOnI4Eh04

Tax Avoidance: http://en.wikipedia.org/wiki/Tax_avoidance
Tax Law: http://en.wikipedia.org/wiki/Income_tax_%28U.S.%29
Without paying (gift tax):
http://en.wikipedia.org/wiki/Gift_tax_in_the_United_States#Gift_tax_exemptions
http://www.irs.gov/Businesses/Small-Businesses-&-Self-Employed/What%27s-New---Estate-and-Gift-Tax
AMT: http://en.wikipedia.org/wiki/Alternative_minimum_tax
Estate planning fun. http://tonyp4idea.blogspot.com/2014/08/estate-planning-101-for-me.html
Taxes on stocks: https://www.youtube.com/watch?v=EKYMbsjUUtE
Tax avoidance: https://www.youtube.com/watch?v=tXou5pM7zh0
Capital gain: https://www.youtube.com/watch?v=ezPs4ibFsNU&t=2678s
Trading course: https://www.youtube.com/watch?v=8sbfrusR5Eo
How safe our brokers. https://www.youtube.com/watch?v=wz64z1YuL0A

Fidelity funds: https://www.youtube.com/watch?v=xdEunmLrhb4
Fidelity core money market fund:
https://www.youtube.com/watch?v=KU6HYRHj3jg

Government bond default? https://www.youtube.com/watch?v=wMxj6iB92ZA
Broker CDs (Recommended): https://www.youtube.com/watch?v=zhEiyW2N7KE
Money market fund: https://www.youtube.com/watch?v=N53wZ_80abU

Economy
YouTube video (highly recommended):
https://www.youtube.com/watch?v=Q6NIDJZdQH4

What will the world be in 5 years (2027).
https://www.youtube.com/watch?v=LzipwDQBUyc

Inflation and interest rate:
https://www.youtube.com/watch?v=q8KJSNyAHLE
Wealth gap widens with low interest rate:
https://www.youtube.com/watch?v=t6m49vNjEGs
Investing helps the economy:
https://www.youtube.com/watch?v=W6ICRTqsxk8

#Filler: Honey, my book can play music.
https://www.youtube.com/watch?v=HxGT5z6d-GA&list=PLMZa6mP7jZ2b1otqG4tfbgZpLEdh6YiNF